# ALMOST HOME

# ALMOST
# HOME

## A Call to Revival and Reformation

# TED N. C. WILSON

Pacific Press® Publishing Association
Nampa, Idaho
Oshawa, Ontario, Canada
www.pacificpress.com

Cover design by Steve Lanto
Cover design resources from dreamstime.com
Inside design by Michelle C. Petz

The author assumes full responsibility for the accuracy of all facts and quotations as cited in this book.

In chapters 1–3, 5, 7, 8, unattributed Bible references are from the King James Version.

Unattributed Bible references in chapters 4 and 9–13 are taken from the New King James Version®. Copyright © 1982 by Thomas Nelson, Inc. Used by permission. All rights reserved.

Unattributed Bible references in chapter 6 are from J. B. Phillips, The New Testament in Modern English, 1962 edition, published by HarperCollins.

You can obtain additional copies of this book by calling toll-free 1-800-765-6955 or by visiting www.adventistbookcenter.com.

Library of Congress Cataloging-in-Publication Data:

Wilson, Ted N. C.
  Almost home : a call to revival and reformation / Ted N.C. Wilson.
    p. cm.
  ISBN 13: 978-0-8163-3597-8 (pbk.)
  ISBN 10: 0-8163-3597-4 (pbk.)
  1. Christian life—Adventist authors. 2. General Conference of
Seventh-day Adventists—Doctrines. I. Title.
  BV4501.3.W5564 2012
  248.4′86732—dc23
                        2012028434

12 13 14 15 16 • 5 4 3 2 1

# Contents

# Foreword

Thinking about books that you shouldn't be without—books that are a must for your library. *Almost Home* is one of those books. Elder Ted Wilson, the president of the General Conference of Seventh-day Adventists, opens his heart about the issues that really matter in these critical times. These messages first appeared as sermons that Elder Wilson preached. In that form, they blessed tens of thousands of people around the world. Now they have been brought together in book form to inspire many more people.

Each chapter will speak to both your mind and your heart. Each will stimulate your thinking, and each will motivate you to recommit your life to the One who died for you and now lives for you. You will be inspired and challenged as you read these pages.

In the chapter titled "Know the Word," Elder Wilson speaks earnestly to each church member, appealing to all of us to saturate our minds with the Word of God. He reminds us of Ellen White's warning that "none but those who have fortified the mind with the truths of the Bible will stand through the last great conflict."[1] I am confident that as you read this chapter, you will feel convicted to place greater priority on your study of God's Word.

In the chapter "Our Only Hope," Elder Wilson presents the righteousness of Jesus as our only hope of salvation. He elevates the unmerited, undeserved grace of Christ in all of its matchless charms, but assures us that though it surpasses in value everything else in the universe, God has made it fully available to each of us.

Elder Wilson's passion to see this lost world won for Christ rings clear in chapters such as "Mission to the Cities" and "Bringing Health to the World." There we can see that the millions who have never had an opportunity to hear God's last-day message are on his heart. He longs to inspire the seventeen million Seventh-day Adventists around the world to reach out in loving acts of kindness to their friends, neighbors, working associates, and families—acts that witness powerfully for Christ and His end-time church.

In the last two chapters of the book, "Faith on Fire!" and "Go Forward!" Elder Wilson urges Adventists everywhere to be ready for the return of our Lord. *Almost Home* is a decidedly Adventist book. Its underlying theme, Christ's soon return, seems to leap off every page. Every chapter aims to help the reader prepare for that day. As you peruse these pages, you will realize anew that Jesus' advent is the only answer to the problems that threaten to overwhelm all who live on this planet. You will find much encouragement in the biblical assurances that Christ has an end-time church that will triumph at last and that one day the glory of God will fill this wayward, troubled world.

It is my hope that as you read this book, you will be drawn closer to the Christ who died for you, who is now in heaven interceding for you, and who will soon come so that where He is, you may be also.

Mark A. Finley
Assistant to the President
General Conference of Seventh-day Adventists

---

1.  Ellen G. White, *The Great Controversy* (Nampa, ID: Pacific Press®, 1950), 593.

# Preface

As we come closer to the very end of time and to Christ's return, we need to rely more and more on Him to supply our every need. We are dependent on Him for our salvation and for our everyday needs. The political, economic, societal, climatic, and ecumenical events around us indicate that He is coming soon. We are almost home! It is time for us to submit ourselves to the Lord and to join our fellow believers in pleading humbly for revival and reformation, recognizing that God has promised to pour out the latter rain of the Holy Spirit so that His work will be finished quickly.

It is our great privilege to dig deeply into our Bibles and to be revived by His Word. It is my fervent hope that, as God instructed in 2 Chronicles 7:14, each of us as members of God's remnant church will humble ourselves, pray earnestly, seek the presence of Christ through His Word, and turn from our own willful desires, allowing the Holy Spirit to control us instead. God wants to use each of us to proclaim by word and act the fullness of the three angels' messages of Revelation 14—Christ, His righteousness, His sanctuary service, His Sabbath, the true worship of God, and Christ's soon return.

What a privilege we have!—we whom God has called to make the greatest proclamation of all time, announcing to the whole world the conclusion of the great controversy between Christ and Satan with the complete assurance that Christ will be victorious. What a privilege to be united in Christ, to serve others in His name, and to share the precious

Seventh-day Adventist message of Bible truth! God is asking us to use every type of outreach possible to share His message with the world.

I invite you to participate in the Seventh-day Adventist Church's many modes of witnessing, including *The Great Controversy* distribution project, Mission to the Cities, medical missionary work, and all other forms of evangelistic outreach. Please help us carry the good news to the millions in the cities and the rural areas. We must witness about Christ in the cities through the methods outlined in the Spirit of Prophecy—the heaven-inspired, blessing-filled writings that God has provided to His church.

In reference to the great challenge of sharing Christ in the cities, Ellen G. White has told us, "There is no change in the messages that God has sent in the past. The work in the cities is the essential work for this time. When the cities are worked as God would have them, the result will be the setting in operation of a mighty movement such as we have not yet witnessed."[1] This is a great burden I have on my heart, and I ask all readers of this book to carry this burden as well. I have dedicated all the royalties from the sales of this book to the comprehensive urban evangelism activities of Mission to the Cities.

May this book draw you to a closer walk with the Lord by pointing you to the Bible, to the Spirit of Prophecy, and to the great task of giving the loud cry that has been entrusted to each of us as members of this great Advent movement.

Ted N. C. Wilson
President
General Conference of Seventh-day Adventists

---

1.    Ellen G. White, *Medical Ministry* (Mountain View, CA: Pacific Press®, 1963), 304.

# CHAPTER 1

# Virtual Reality

A generation ago, technological gadgets were mostly just conversation pieces. People didn't buy them because they were particularly useful; they got them for curiosity's sake or to show how far ahead of the crowd they were.

Now, however, technological gadgets have become virtual necessities. We expect the vehicles we drive to have backup cameras and the "books" we read to give us access to all virtual encyclopedias. And job-wise, we could hardly function, never mind compete, without our smart phones and tablets, which not only keep us in constant touch with everyone in our lives but also hold our to-do lists and appointment and address books.

Of course, our military forces use night-vision goggles and laser-guided missiles and pilotless drones that not only spy on and bomb the enemy, but also can out-fly—and shoot down—manned fighter planes. And those in the know report that in the near future, 50 percent of all tanks and other assault vehicles will be remotely controlled.

Then there's virtual reality. That's the use of technology (visual and auditory) to make people feel they're somewhere else doing something else—playing tennis, for instance. Or flying a plane or driving a race car or checking out a house plan by virtually walking through a house built on that plan. Virtual reality is used in computer games, military and aviation training, graphic design, life-experience simulation, spatial tours of almost anything, and much more.

Virtual reality—*almost real*, but not quite.

In these strange and uncertain times, we might ask whether technology has so shaped our view of the universe that we think of God as existing only as virtual reality. Do we create a virtual Jesus—one whom we can manipulate and craft to our own liking? One whom we can keep in a box and pull out only when we need him or want him?

Some people don't want even a virtual Jesus. They don't want *any* kind of Jesus at all.

But Jesus is a real Person who wants to have a real relationship with us. God created human beings in His image (see Genesis 1:26). If we're like Him, then what we are tells us something of what He is. And since we're real rather than virtual beings, He must be too.

Yes, God is a real person who enjoyed coming "in the cool of the day" and talking with the man and woman He made (Genesis 3:8). And after Adam and Eve sinned, our real God spoke to the real devil and revealed the very real outcome of the conflict that was affecting everyone in the universe. He said, "I will put enmity between thee [the devil] and the woman, and between thy seed and her seed; it shall bruise thy head, and thou shalt bruise his heel" (Genesis 3:15). Here, as other scriptures make clear (see, e.g., Galatians 3:16), God was announcing that a real Christ would really become human and would eventually destroy the one who brought sin and death into what had been a perfect home, a perfect universe.

## "That I may dwell among them"

Even before His birth, Christ mingled with His people, speaking to the patriarchs, standing between the Israelites and their enemy, meeting Moses on Mount Sinai, and telling him, "Let them make me a sanctuary; that I may dwell among them [the Israelites]" (Exodus 25:8).

So the children of Israel built a sanctuary where God met with His people. However, although the sanctuary was made of real linen and wood and bronze and gold, it was, in a sense, virtual reality. It was a representation of the real sanctuary, which is in heaven. Ellen White said, "That sanctuary, in which Jesus ministers in our behalf, is the great original, of which the sanctuary built by Moses was a copy."[1]

The book of Hebrews calls the heavenly sanctuary "the true tabernacle, which the Lord pitched, and not man" (Hebrews 8:2). The heavenly and earthly sanctuaries both pictured a real God, in His love, demonstrating how He intended to save us. They pointed to Christ, the Lamb who died for us—who died in our place. They pointed to Christ, the High Priest mediating for His people; to Christ, who conquered sin—which shows the ultimate glory of the sanctuary services. As Ellen White put it, because of the sanctuary, people's "minds were carried forward to the closing events of the great controversy between Christ and Satan, the final purification of the universe from sin and sinners."[2]

The sanctuary was pointing to the real Jesus, who would live a real life and conquer real sin by dying. He wouldn't die on a sanitized cross, a virtual cross, a graphically retouched cross. No, He would die on a real, rough instrument of torture in real agony that He could bear only by depending on the strength of His heavenly Father. This very real Jesus rose from His stony grave and ascended to a real heaven to serve as a real High Priest in the real heavenly sanctuary.

There's nothing virtual about the salvation God worked out for us. It's all real—real love, real mercy, and a real sacrifice! Can you imagine the horror of Adam and Eve back in Eden as they cut the throat of a perfect lamb so they could have forgiveness (Leviticus 5:5, 6)? No virtual reality there. They were dealing with real stuff—stuff that pointed to the real death of Jesus for you and me. Paul tells us that "without shedding of blood is no remission" (Hebrews 9:22). Real soldiers with real weapons really shed Christ's blood. He paid the ultimate sacrifice to conquer sin so we could have eternal life.

Christ not only became the ultimate sacrifice on our behalf, but when He returned to heaven He also began to act as our Mediator and High Priest. Look at Hebrews 9:24. There Paul says, "Christ is not entered into the holy places made with hands, which are the figures of the true; but into heaven itself, now to appear in the presence of God for us." So there is a real Christ appearing before God right now for you and me.

How is it that He has the right to represent us before God? Paul said that Christ came "to put away sin by the sacrifice of himself. . . . So Christ was once offered to bear the sins of many; and unto them that look for him shall he appear the second time without sin unto salvation" (verses 26–28). Ellen White tells us: "Christ was appointed to the office of Mediator from the creation of God, set up from everlasting to be our substitute and surety."[3]

And God developed this plan for our salvation before He created the world. Can't you hear the hush in the galactic war room in heaven as the plan was unveiled? The Supreme Authority spoke with unwavering commitment: "We will provide salvation for every person who is willing to submit his or her life to the Lord Jesus Christ."

What an incredible God we serve!

This incredible God has commissioned us to use the Internet and every other means possible to tell everyone we can that God wants everyone who has faith, who trusts Him, to live with Him forever, and He has done all that's necessary to make that possible. God has asked us to present the reality of Jesus, of salvation from sin and death, of Jesus' soon coming, and to invite people to choose to serve Him.

## God's covenant with us

To those who humbly commit themselves to God, He says, "This is the covenant that I will make with them after those days, . . . I will put my laws into their hearts, and in their minds will I write them; and their sins and iniquities will I remember no more" (Hebrews 10:16, 17, quoting Jeremiah 31:33, 34). And in verses 19–23, Paul tells us that Jesus' blood was shed for us so we may have "boldness to enter into the holiest"; and because there is now a High Priest serving the house of God (which includes us), we should "draw near with a true heart in full assurance of faith." Paul says that since we can have faith in a real God who has provided salvation for us, we are to "hold fast the profession of our faith without wavering; (for he is faithful that promised)."

So how do we connect with this God? How, in a world of virtual reality, do we find the real thing?

In a poem titled "Did Jesus Use a Modem at the Sermon on the Mount?" Ellis Bush considers the reality of Jesus and of what He's done for us and the question of how we connect with Him. Near the end of his poem he asks, "Have the wonders of this modern age / Made you question what is true? / How a single man, in a simple time / Could offer life anew?" Then he gives his answer: "If in your life, the voice of God / Is sometimes hard to hear; . . . Then set aside your laptop . . . / And all the fancy gear, / Open your Bible, open your heart, / And let the Lord draw near."[4]

There's no virtual reality in the story of Jesus and what He's done for our salvation. Jesus is real. His love for us is real. His life, death, and resurrection were real. His mediation in the heavenly sanctuary is real. And the mission He's given us—that of sharing this wonderful story with others through both what we say and what we do—is real.

Let me tell you about someone who knows God is real. I was in Londonderry, Northern Ireland, a while ago. The Protestants and Catholics there live in an uneasy truce. I could feel the tension in the air, and the fully armed British soldiers on patrol and the fortresslike defenses around the police and military stations gave it substance. What I saw told me clearly that I was in a tough place.

At that time we had a number of active church members in Derry. They worshiped in a church built by Maranatha Volunteers in 1978. I met a wonderful saint named Anna in that church. She'd been an Adventist for about thirty years, having learned about and accepted the Advent message through Voice of Prophecy lessons. She believes in a real God and the real power of prayer.

Back in 1978, when the church was built, there were about thirty-five members in Derry. But over time, people have moved away, died, or become discouraged and stopped attending, and eventually, Anna was the only one left in the church. One could almost have called it a virtual church, but it was still real because Anna kept coming every Sabbath.

The Irish Mission wanted to close the church and sell the building. But Anna steadfastly opposed that, demanding that the Mission keep sending a preacher each Sabbath. She kept coming Sabbath after Sabbath, insisting that her atheistic husband drive her there though he protested every kilometer of the way. And she kept praying that the Lord would send more people to the church—to the church and to the message she loved. But no one came.

Then one Sabbath, Anna prayed, "Lord, send at least one person to the church," and the very next Sabbath, Mary showed up!

Mary was a native of Derry, but she had gone to Canada, where she met and married Ross. While living in Toronto, they became Adventists, and sometime after that they decided to move to Derry.

Mary got there a few weeks before Ross did, and when the Sabbath came, she decided she would go to church. She expected to find lots of people there, as had been the case in Toronto, but she found only one person—Anna. That may have disappointed Mary, but having a fellow worshiper thrilled Anna. God answered her prayer! Ross soon joined them, and several others have too, so about twelve people attend the church regularly—including Ann, Mary's sister.

The few Adventists who live in Derry face a tough life every day now. But they know that God is real, and they're looking forward to the fellowship they'll have with Christ when He comes the second time. They're anticipating a real Second Coming.

Not a hologram.

Not some kind of wide-screen TV wizardry.

Not virtual reality.

The real thing.

Soon we'll see a small dark cloud about half the size of a man's hand. It will grow larger and larger and brighter and brighter till it fills the whole sky. That "cloud" will be composed of billions of angels, with the very real Jesus Christ—the One who died for all of us—seated right in the center! All heaven has come to see in person the victory God has won. And 1 John 3:2 says, "When he shall appear, we shall be like him; for we shall see him as he is." This same Jesus who made us in His image—we will see Him as is He is: *REAL!*

Jesus has called us to tell others that He is real. He offers us the power and the guidance of the Holy Spirit to enable us to witness for Him. Let's commit ourselves to sharing Him on the Internet, in our lives, and every other way we can. He is our Lord and Creator. Our Redeemer and Mediator. Our Friend and our very real King.

He's not a fake. He's not a virtual person. He's real! And we're almost home.

---

1.   Ellen G. White, *Patriarchs and Prophets* (Oakland, CA: Pacific Press®, 1890), 357.

2.   Ibid., 358.

3.   Ellen G. White, *Selected Messages* (Washington, DC: Review and Herald®, 1958), 1:250.

4.   Ellis Bush Jr., *Did Jesus Use a Modem at the Sermon on the Mount? Inspirational Thoughts for the Information Age* (Mukilteo, WA: WinePress, 1997), 8.

# CHAPTER 2

# Know the Word

We're facing a crisis. It's about the Bible. Do Seventh-day Adventists consider the Bible to be God's Word, or do we think it's just a collection of nice recommendations and sayings? Is it our handbook for living, or is it merely something to display on the living-room table? Is the Bible authoritative, or is it not?

The psalmist said, "Thy word have I hid in mine heart, that I might not sin against thee" (Psalm 119:11). When he wrote "Thy word," he was talking about God's Word. Are we Adventists actively reading God's Word and allowing it to speak to our hearts and through us to others, or are we ignoring the Word?

I have many versions of the Bible in my home, and I've had ones that I particularly loved—King James Versions in which I had underlined sections, cross-referenced passages, and written many notes. No doubt that's why I treasured those particular Bibles. One of them was ruined as we landed in a downpour in the middle of Congo. Sheets of water flowed across the underside of a mission airplane and worked their way through the skin of the plane and into the suitcase where I had placed that Bible. I searched for another one like it and used it for years. When the cover gave out, I had it rebound. But I lost it recently—I left it on an airplane in South Africa. I now have another study Bible version and am trying to get used to it.

I love my Bible—it's my friend! You probably feel the same way about your Bible.

Francis Schaeffer, noted Christian leader, author, and founder of L'Abri Christian retreat center in Switzerland, once said that he loved his Bible so much and it gave him such comfort, such assurance that he kept it close to him. He kept it close enough that when he was lying on his bed in the dark, he could reach out and touch it.

During my family's stay in Russia, we noticed how much people there respected and appreciated the Bible. Before the fall of Communism, Bibles were scarce—scarce enough that people were willing to risk smuggling them into the country. After Russia gave its people religious freedom, Bibles were more readily available, but Russian Christians still treasured their Bibles. Just holding a Bible brought them joy.

Of course, we don't believe in "bibliolatry." We don't worship the Bible. We worship the Word that was made flesh—Jesus Christ, our Lord. It isn't the book itself that is really important; it's what's *in* the book.

Seventh-day Adventists have long treasured the Bible and have been called "people of the Book." Prophecy indicates that, by God's grace, in the future we will again be known as "people of the Book." But do our friends know us as "people of the Book" right now? Are we actively using the Bible, or are we just pretending we are committed Christians?

Roy Robertson, who together with Dawson Trotman founded the Christian group the Navigators, said an experience he had at the beginning of World War II showed him that he was faking it spiritually. His ship, the USS *West Virginia*, docked in Pearl Harbor on December 6, 1941. Robertson went ashore with a couple of other sailors and dropped in on a Bible study.

The leader of the study said he wanted everyone there to recite their favorite Bible verse and tell what it meant to them. That terrified Robertson. He had grown up in a Christian home and had gone to church three times a week, but he couldn't think of a single verse. Eventually, he remembered John 3:16—but then the sailor whose turn came just before Robertson recited and commented on that famous verse. Robertson said he couldn't come up with another verse, so he sat there in stunned humiliation. And when he went to bed that night, the thought that he was a spiritual fake kept running through his mind.

At 7:55 the next morning, the ship alarm awakened him with the call to man the battle stations. That was the day of the Japanese attack on Pearl Harbor.

Robertson and his crew raced to their machine gun emplacement, but they had no real bullets there; all they had was practice ammunition. So for the first fifteen minutes of the two-hour-long battle, they were firing blanks—and hoping they could at least scare the Japanese pilots away from their ship.

Robertson said that as he fired that fake ammunition, he thought, *Roy, this is what you've been doing your whole life—firing blanks for Christ.* Then, as the Japanese bullets slammed into his ship, he made up his mind that if he escaped with his life, he would get serious about following Jesus.

As Adventists coming to the end of time, have we become so complacent that all we're doing is firing blanks for Jesus? Are we serious about following Christ and digging into the Word? Are we just pretending to be "people of the Book," or does God's Word mean something special to us—special enough that we are sharing it with others?

# Dusty Bibles

Recently, a sign that I drive past outside of a church not far from our home had a message that caught my attention. It said, "Dusty Bibles lead to dirty lives." Have we become so busy that our Bibles are dusty? Have we forgotten our roots as "people of the Book"—people commissioned to proclaim the last-day Advent message from the Bible?

Ellen White's *Selected Messages,* volume 2, is a favorite book of mine. The Spirit of Prophecy is such a great blessing to this church corporately and individually. Note what Ellen White has to say about the Word of God in the end times.

> We have need now for more than human wisdom in reading and searching the Scriptures; and if we come to God's Word with humble hearts, He will raise up a standard for us against the lawless element. . . .

When men press close to the side of Jesus, when Christ is abiding in their hearts by faith, their love for the commandments of God grows stronger. . . .

It is at this time that the true Sabbath must be brought before the people by both pen and voice. As the fourth commandment and those who observe it are ignored and despised, the faithful feel that it is the time not to hide their faith but to exalt the law of Jehovah by unfurling the banner on which is inscribed the message of the third angel, the commandments of God and the faith of Jesus.[1]

Signs in the world indicate that Christ's second coming is imminent. The Bible will become more and more important as the end of time unfolds. It is God's Word, and it's pointing to the Living Word—Jesus Christ—and His plan for this earth and our lives.

Many of the Jews who lived in Thessalonica weren't willing to dig deeply into the Word and allow the gospel to transform their lives. Instead, they conspired together and started a riot. Afraid of being blamed as the cause of the uproar, the Thessalonian believers sent Paul and Silas at nighttime to Berea. There they found kind, open-minded Jews who were willing to listen to the apostles' preaching about Jesus and then to dig into the Scriptures to see whether or not what they heard was right. Luke wrote that the Bereans "were more noble than those in Thessalonica, in that they received the word with all readiness of mind, and searched the scriptures daily, whether those things were so" (Acts 17:11).

The truth became real to the Bereans. They didn't depend on someone else or fake their commitment to serving God. "Daily they searched the inspired records, and as they compared scripture with scripture, heavenly angels were beside them, enlightening their minds and impressing their hearts."[2]

Today, heavenly angels are by our sides, opening our minds as we prayerfully study the Scriptures. The Holy Spirit can then point us to Christ, the Living Word, who brings conviction and conversion.

We are living in the last days, in the Laodicean period, when we can easily fake our Christianity. The devil will use every means to distract us from the Bible and what it teaches: recreation, television, amusements, work, music, squabbles, false teachings, discord, economic problems— anything that will occupy our time and keep us away from God's Word.

There's something else that poses a great danger to us because it distracts us from digging into the Word the way the Bereans did. It's called "experiential religion." Its proponents claim that you have to "feel" the Spirit. Religion must be "experienced" to be real. Thus people's feelings, their emotions, are taking over much of the religious world. What happens to faith in Christ and His Word when people give primary attention to how they feel? What happens when they don't "feel" like being religious? What happens when they don't "feel" close to God? What happens when they act more like the Thessalonians than the Bereans— paying more attention to their feelings than to searching the Bible?

Ellen White warned, "In the last days, the earth will be almost destitute of true faith. Upon the merest pretense, the word of God will be considered unreliable, while human reasoning will be received, though it be in opposition to plain Scripture facts."[3]

You see, feelings lie. We can know the truth only as we base it on the authority of Scripture. God's Word never lies. It is always dependable.

Paul reminded Timothy of the value of Scripture, saying that Holy Scripture can make people "wise unto salvation through faith which is in Christ Jesus" (2 Timothy 3:15). The apostle went on to say, "All scripture is given by inspiration of God, and is profitable for doctrine, for reproof, for correction, for instruction in righteousness: That the man of God may be perfect, thoroughly furnished unto all good works" (verses 16, 17).

Ellen White also said,

We are standing upon the very borders of the eternal world. Fair-weather Christians will not be wanted for this work. The sentimental and tasteful religion is not needed for this time. There must be intensity brought into our faith and in the proclamation of truth.[4]

The Bible can create in us that intensity of faith and witness. It does so by giving us a clear understanding of the commission God has given to the Seventh-day Adventist Church—that of proclaiming the three angels' messages to the entire world. The Bible rings true. God's Word is powerful.

# Time well spent

Studying the Bible and eternal values brings physical and mental benefits that spending time on trivial things doesn't offer. Ellen White noted,

> Thousands are today in the insane asylum whose minds became unbalanced by novel reading, which results in . . . lovesick sentimentalism. The Bible is the book of books. It will give you life and health. It is a soother of the nerves, and imparts solidity of mind and firm principle.[5]

Some years ago, my father-in-law, Dr. Don Vollmer, had a patient, Phil Collins, who wasn't a church member. Phil's father had been the director of the Mint in Washington, DC, and Phil himself was a retired civil servant who as a young man had been a schoolmate if not a classmate of J. Edgar Hoover in law school. In his retirement, Phil asked Dad Vollmer what he could do to prevent mental deterioration. Dad told him that the best way to keep his mind sharp was to read the Bible. Uncle Phil, as he was known to the Vollmer family, did just that—and read himself into the Adventist Church! He became a close friend of the Vollmer family and a faithful member of the Foster Memorial Seventh-day Adventist Church in Asheville, North Carolina. His mind stayed alert and sharp nearly up to his death in his early nineties.

Arthur Maxwell tells the story of a rich farmer in ancient Greece who, on his deathbed, said to his sons, "My treasure is buried in my fields. If you would be rich, dig for it."

The sons presumed their father had put his money in an ironbound chest and buried it somewhere on his farm, so they set out eagerly to find it. They turned over the soil in all their fields, using every kind of digging tool they owned and digging to a depth no plow had ever reached. But they found no sign of the treasure chest.

In the spring, the sons abandoned their search so the fields could be planted with wheat. Summer came, and then the harvest—and what a harvest it was! They had never had such an incredible crop! Digging the land so thoroughly had produced the riches they sought. The plan their wise old father devised had succeeded!

We also have inherited a fortune, but ours is buried in the Bible. We need to search the that holy Book as thoroughly as those two sons searched their fields—as thoroughly as the Bereans searched Scripture, digging into it with all the spiritual tools we have. When we do, we'll find real treasure, for the Word of God brings us face to face with the greatest Treasure—Jesus Christ, our Savior.

The Bible will reveal that we can obtain salvation only through complete reliance on Christ—on His life and death, His resurrection, and on the ministry He's carrying on for us in the Most Holy Place of the heavenly sanctuary. It will tell us that the Sabbath is Christ's special seal and covenant with His commandment-keeping people. And it will confirm our belief and hope in a literal second coming of Christ, our Redeemer, and that He will come soon.

# With what motives?

I found a poem titled "How Readest Thou?"[6] in a Bible that had belonged to my mother. The first two lines say, "It is one thing to read the Bible through, / Another thing to read, and learn, and do." Then this poem points out numerous motives people have for reading the Bible, such as to fulfill a duty, to enhance their reputation, to copy what their neighbors do, to find contradictions, to prove beliefs they already hold, and so forth.

How do you go about reading the Bible? Do you read it to find Christ and His truth, or do you read it for other reasons? It's important that we read God's Word in the right way and for the right reasons, because what it says is crucial to our surviving the troubles of the end-times. The Bible will strengthen our belief that we serve a God who will never fail and whose church will triumph over the attacks of the devil. We are facing those attacks already, but they will increase. The church will be deluged with apostasies and false doctrine. But the Word of God stands sure!

Ellen White warns,

> We are living in the perils of the last days. A superficial faith results in a superficial experience. . . . All should see the necessity of understanding the truth for themselves individually. . . . There is great need to search the book of Daniel and the book of Revelation, and learn the texts thoroughly. . . .
>
> Apostasies have occurred and the Lord has permitted matters of this nature to develop in the past in order to show how easily His people will be misled when they depend upon the words of men instead of searching the Scriptures for themselves, as did the noble Bereans, to see if these things are so.[7]

We will be able to stand the test only if we follow the lead of the Bereans, since the Bible is the only foundation that will prove sturdy enough to build our faith on. Satan will do everything to destroy the confidence of Seventh-day Adventists in the landmark truths we have held dear, but he will not succeed. Christ's church will never be broken or destroyed. The devil has tried all sorts of things to eliminate God's church without success.

In the year AD 360, Flavius Claudius Julianus (Julian) ascended the throne as Caesar. He was the nephew of Constantine the Great, who "Christianized" the Roman world. Julian sought to re-establish pagan worship in the empire and was thereafter known as "Julian the Apostate." He began to openly persecute Christians, whom he called "Galileans," and he withdrew the legal protection Constantine had granted them.

Julian had been educated in Athens alongside a committed Christian by the name of Agaton. Although Julian persecuted Christians, he invited his friend Agaton to serve in his court. Julian frequently teased this friend. One day, in front of a large group of wealthy Romans, Julian asked, "Agaton, how is your carpenter of Nazareth? Is he finding work these days?"

Agaton smiled and answered, "He is perhaps taking time away from building mansions for the faithful to build a coffin for your empire."

Less than two years later, on June 26, 363, Julian lay dying from a Persian spear wound in his abdomen. He had led his troops in an attempt to take the ancient Persian Empire. Julian grasped a handful of dust that was red with his blood. Flinging the dust heavenward, he uttered his last words: "*Vicisti, Galilaee*"—that is, "You have conquered, Galilean." The Roman Empire has long since crumbled into the dust of history, but the empire of the Carpenter lives on and will continue to live till His glorious second coming and beyond, into eternity.

The Lord wants His people to be the champions of truth through His power. We should remember "that the church, enfeebled and defective though it be, is the only object on earth on which Christ bestows His supreme regard."[8] We are to lift up the banner of Christ and proclaim the distinctive biblical message He has given us for this hour.

A few pages back in *Selected Messages*, we read,

> We are Seventh-day Adventists, and of this name we are never to be ashamed. As a people we must take a firm stand for truth and righteousness. . . . We must look ever to Jesus, the Author and Finisher of our faith. . . .
>
> I was told that men will employ every policy to make less prominent the difference between the faith of Seventh-day Adventists and those who observe the first day of the week. In this controversy the whole world will be engaged, and the time is short. This is no time to haul down our colors.[9]

By God's grace, let us champion the Word of God and exalt Christ, who is the Word. Let us look to the Bible for life, and let us make it the foundation of our belief. We are facing a battle, and we must know what we believe in.

# Proving their genuineness

Some years ago, when the Sandinistas were active and powerful in Nicaragua, a pastor and a church elder were traveling to a remote mountain area to minister to members of our church who lived there. A Sandinista officer backed up by 120 soldiers stopped them and ordered them to get out of the car. The officer searched the car, brought out a Bible and a hymnal, and asked, "Where are you going?" The pastor told him, but the officer said he didn't believe him. "You're just spies," he said. Generally, the Sandinistas made people they thought to be spies to dig their own graves and then shot them.

The officer paged through the hymnal. "Do you know this song, 'Take My Life and Let It Be'?" he asked.

"Yes, we do," they replied.

"OK, then sing it," ordered the officer.

So, the pastor and church elder sang a duet, which touched the hearts of the soldiers.

Next, the officer picked up the Bible and opened it. "Do you know Psalm 91?" he asked.

"Yes, I do," said the pastor.

"Then repeat it," demanded the officer.

So the pastor repeated Psalm 91.

The officer was impressed but still had doubts. He picked out several more chapters, such as John 14 and 1 Corinthians 13, and asked the pastor about them. Then he found Matthew 4, which tells about Christ's calling of the disciples.

"Do you know this story?" asked the officer.

"Yes, I do," replied the pastor.

"Then preach us a sermon," ordered the officer.

The pastor preached powerfully for fifteen or twenty minutes and then brought his sermon to a heart-searching conclusion. He said, "This story didn't end with the disciples. Christ wants all people everywhere to follow Him." Then he appealed to the soldiers to follow Christ, bringing tears to the eyes of the hardened soldiers.

When the pastor had finished preaching, the officer said he was fully persuaded that the two men were who they claimed to be. He said, "If you hadn't been able to prove you were Christians, we would have killed you." Then the officer confessed that he had once been a Christian and believed the Bible, but he had lost his faith. He said, "I admire you, and I believe you can help our people. In the future, whenever you need to go up into the mountains, contact me, and I'll send soldiers to go with you because it's dangerous for you to go there alone."

It pays to know the Bible and to know what you believe. The Bible contains the messages God wants us and all people everywhere to receive. It is the only anchor we can depend upon as we face the uncertainties of the future.

Jesus is coming soon, but before He returns, the devil will counterfeit even *that* incredible event. We won't be able to believe even what we see with our own eyes; we'll have to hang our faith entirely on the Word of God.

So, search the Scriptures daily.

Know the Word.

Cherish it.

Read it.

Believe it.

Preach it.

Share it.

And love it.

Allow the Bible to live in your life. As Paul wrote, "Let the word of Christ dwell in you richly" (Colossians 3:16).

We're almost home. As members of God's great Advent movement, let's overcome the Laodicean crisis by hiding God's Word in our hearts and becoming "people of the Book." And empowered by the Holy Spirit, let us share God's Word with others.

1.　Ellen G. White, *Selected Messages* (Washington, DC: Review and Herald®, 1958), 2:367–369.

2.　Ellen G. White, *The Acts of the Apostles* (Mountain View, CA: Pacific Press®, 1911), 231, 232.

3.　Ellen G. White, *The Spirit of Prophecy* (Oakland, CA: Pacific Press®, 1884), 1:89.

4.　White, *Selected Messages*, 2:382.

5.　Ellen G. White, *Counsels on Sabbath School Work* (Washington, DC: Review and Herald®, 1938), 22, 23.

6.　Author unknown.

7.　White, *Selected Messages*, 2:392–394.

8.　Ibid., 396.

9.　Ibid., 384, 385.

# CHAPTER 3

# God's Magnificent Gift

T he very last deception of Satan will be to make of none effect the testimony of the Spirit of God. . . . Satan will work ingeniously, in different ways and through different agencies, to unsettle the confidence of God's remnant people in the true testimony."[1]

"Soon every possible effort will be made to discount and pervert the truth of the testimonies of God's Spirit. We must have in readiness the clear, straight messages that since 1846 have been coming to God's people."[2]

Ellen White is very clear, isn't she? When we're almost home, when the world is heading into the final battle of the great controversy, Satan will try to derail God's people by shaking their confidence in "the testimony of the Spirit of God"—in the Spirit of Prophecy, in other words. Why? What makes the Spirit of Prophecy such a threat to Satan that he fights it to the very end?

Scripture equates the Spirit of Prophecy with the testimony of Jesus (see Revelation 19:10). The testimony of our Lord. The testimony of the divine Being who took the form of a servant and then humbled Himself even more, to the point of dying on a cross (see Philippians 2). This Lord, who is the Word made flesh (see John 1) and who gave us the Holy Scripture, has also given us the Spirit of Prophecy.

Don't get the wrong impression. I'm not saying that the Spirit of Prophecy is the Bible or is equal to the Bible. As Ellen White indicates, the role of the Spirit of Prophecy is not to replace the Bible, but to lead people to the Bible. However, it's important that we understand that the Spirit of Prophecy is the product of the same heavenly inspiration that gave us the Bible. After all, like the Bible, it is the testimony of Jesus.

Ellen White tells us,

> Through His Holy Spirit the voice of God has come to us continually in warning and instruction, to confirm the faith of the believers in the Spirit of prophecy. Repeatedly the word has come, Write the things that I have given you to confirm the faith of My people in the position they have taken. Time and trial have not made void the instruction given, but through years of suffering and self-sacrifice have established the truth of the testimony given. The instruction that was given in the early days of the message is to be held as safe instruction to follow in these its closing days.[3]

This testimony of Jesus, the Spirit of Prophecy, is part and parcel of the Advent movement. It is God's magnificent gift to us! It is centered in Christ and all that He represents—His salvation, His grace, and the ministry He's carrying on in the Most Holy Place of the heavenly sanctuary. The Spirit of Prophecy shares what Jesus wants the people waiting for His second coming to know. We don't know just when He will return; Jesus said only the Father knows that. But we do know that He will come very soon. I believe that with all my heart. After all, everything happening in this old world tells us the final events of the great controversy are about to take place.

# Caller ID

My intention isn't so much to convince you that the Spirit of Prophecy is true as it is to point out that the Spirit of Prophecy is relevant now, as the Second Advent draws nigh. In fact, it's God's "Caller ID" for His church—it's one of the identifying characteristics of the remnant church.

Caller ID is great. My wife, Nancy, loves it because knowing who's calling gives her the options of answering the call or letting it go to voicemail. A couple of my daughters even have unique ringtones for some of the people who call them. That way they can tell who's calling by the ringtone they're hearing.

Revelation 12:17 is the great Caller ID of God's remnant people. It says, "The dragon [the serpent, the devil, Satan; see verse 9] was wroth with the woman [God's church], and went to make war with the remnant of her seed [God's last-day people and church], which keep the commandments of God, and have the testimony of Jesus Christ."

So, God's people of the end times will have two prominent characteristics. First, they will be keeping the commandments of God, including the pivotal fourth commandment. That commandment identifies who God is (the Creator of the universe), and keeping it expresses people's allegiance to Him. This holy day is a sign and seal that binds God's people to God Himself for eternity. Ellen White indicated that the Sabbath will play an important role in the events of the last days: "The Sabbath question is to be the issue in the great final conflict in which all the world will act a part. . . . God has called us to uplift the standard of His downtrodden Sabbath."[4]

The Sabbath is the special weekly day of rest sanctified by God Himself and noted in Genesis 2 at the end of creation and re-emphasized in the Ten Commandments given at Mount Sinai. It is integral to our faith and even to our name.

Recently, I had a committed member of our church ask me whether we were purposely downplaying the "seventh-day" aspect of our faith since many of us use the word *Adventist* without prefacing it with *Seventh-day*. I assured him we weren't intentionally downplaying *Seventh-day*, but I also told him that I agree with him that we ought to use our full name wherever and whenever possible. The seventh day is of great importance because Sabbath-keeping represents the kind of relationship with Christ that He wants us to have. Sabbath-keeping isn't a legalistic mechanism for getting people into heaven. Rather, it's a sign of our love and allegiance to our Creator and Redeemer.

The second characteristic of God's remnant church is that it will have the "testimony of Jesus." Revelation 19:10 tells us that is the "spirit of prophecy." The Spirit of Prophecy is a magnificent gift from the Lord, who is the source of inspiration. In a research paper titled "Identifying Marks of the Remnant Church," Gerhard Pfandl explains that "in . . . Revelation 1:2, 9; 12:17, and 20:4 the expression 'testimony of Jesus' is each time balanced symmetrically with the expression 'the word of God' or the phrase 'the commandments of God.'"[5] In other words, the commandments of God and the testimony of Jesus—the Spirit of Prophecy—come from the same source—heaven.

Dr. Pfandl goes on to say,

> The parallelism between the "Word of God" or "the command-ments of God" and the "testimony of Jesus" is vital for an under-standing of the latter expression. "The Word of God" in John's time referred to the Old Testament, and the "testimony of Jesus" to what Jesus had said in the Gospels and through His prophets, like Peter and Paul.[6]

So Revelation 12:17 tells us that in the last days of earth's history God will communicate with His remnant people through the testimony of Jesus/the Spirit of Prophecy. We believe this was fulfilled through the work and writings of the weakest of the weak, Ellen G. White.

In an article published in the *Adventist Review,* Juan Carlos Viera, retired secretary of the Ellen G White Estate, stated,

> The expression "testimony of Jesus" speaks of a loving Savior who wants to maintain communication and close fellowship with us. It tells us that Jesus lies at the center of the gift and that through it He wants to continue a special divine connection with us forever.[7]

The Spirit of Prophecy was given to nurture and assist this last-day movement through providing instruction from heaven. God used the Spirit of Prophecy to guide in the establishment of a remnant people, the Seventh-day Adventist Church, that would love Him supremely and obey His commandments. He used the Spirit of Prophecy, communicated through Ellen White, to nurture this fledgling group into growth that has resulted in multiple millions of members around the world.

## Mere indifference

Why have many Adventists not followed the counsel of God recorded in the writings of the Spirit of Prophecy? It isn't necessarily that they feel animosity toward it, although some people do. The greatest problem is mere indifference. People don't follow God's counsel as given through the Spirit of Prophecy because they aren't acquainted with it. They don't read it, or they ignore what they read in it.

Ellen White counsels,

> The volumes of *Spirit of Prophecy* [forerunner of the Conflict of the Ages series] and also the *Testimonies*, should be introduced into every Sabbathkeeping family, and the brethren should know their value and be urged to read them. It was not the wisest plan to place these books at a low figure and have only one set in a church. They should be in the library of every family and read again and again. Let them be kept where they can be read by many, and let them be worn out in being read by all the neighbors. . . . You should lend *Spirit of Prophecy* to your neighbors and prevail upon them to buy copies for themselves.[8]

In fact, Ellen White said something to the effect that the Conflict of the Ages series "should be placed in every family in the land."[9] This is what our publishing houses and literature evangelists are doing, and what all of us should be doing.

The Spirit of Prophecy has been instrumental in getting God's people involved in publishing, health, and education as aids to fulfilling the mission God has given us. The Spirit of Prophecy has initiated and guided the pastoral, evangelistic, missionary, and administrative expansion of the church. In fact, the writings of the Spirit of Prophecy contain counsel on just about every aspect of life, including theology, lifestyle, personal health, the family, the home, young people, interpersonal relationships, personal stewardship, and more. This divine agency is still guiding God's people, and it will continue to do so until the Lord returns.

The Seventh-day Adventist Church is not just another denomination. It is a heaven-born movement that has a divine destiny: it is to proclaim to the world the three angels' messages. Ellen White tells us that

> in a special sense Seventh-day Adventists have been set in the world as watchmen and light bearers. To them has been entrusted the last warning for a perishing world. On them is shining wonderful light from the Word of God. They have been given a work of the most solemn import—the proclamation of the first, second, and third angels' messages. There is no other work of so great importance. They are to allow nothing else to absorb their attention.[10]

Since the Spirit of Prophecy is to play such a vital role in God's last-day church, is it any wonder that Satan attacks it? Note the following warnings:

> There will be a hatred kindled against the testimonies which is satanic. The workings of Satan will be to unsettle the faith of the churches in them, for this reason: Satan cannot have so clear a track to bring in his deceptions and bind up souls in his delusions if the warnings and reproofs and counsels of the Spirit of God are heeded.[11]

> We must follow the directions given through the Spirit of Prophecy. We must love and obey the truth for this time. This will save us from accepting strong delusions. God has spoken to us through the testimonies to the church, and through the books that have helped to make plain our present duty and the position that we should now occupy.[12]

What is this position that "we should now occupy"? Through the blood and grace of Jesus Christ, He has called us to be the "remnant of her seed"—a unique movement of destiny that is to stand firm for Christ and the truth; to proclaim this Advent message; to bear the testimony of Jesus; to turn people's eyes to Jesus, who is the center of all truth; and through the power of the Holy Spirit, to turn people back to a true worship of Him.

We are to lift up Jesus. Ellen White says,

> Our faith increases by beholding Jesus, who is the center of all that is attractive and lovely. The more we contemplate the heavenly, the less we see desirable and attractive in the earthly. The more continually we fix the eye of faith on Christ, in whom our hopes of eternal life are centered, the more our faith grows.[13]

We must realize that the church is called to do a great work among its members and to those still outside its doors. The shaking and sifting time is coming. It will prepare God's people for the final loud cry, in which Christ has called us to engage. Lift up Christ and His Word. Accept the magnificent gift of the Spirit of Prophecy as we head into the final days of earth's history. Under the Holy Spirit's guidance, the Word of God and the Spirit of Prophecy will bring us to complete humility at the foot of the cross. Then God will be able to do His work, preparing His people for the unbelievable events just ahead.

# What lies ahead

Ellen White describes events that are yet to happen:

> I was shown the people of God, and saw them mightily shaken. Some, with strong faith and agonizing cries, were pleading with God. . . .
>
> Some . . . seemed indifferent and careless. . . .
>
> I asked the meaning of the shaking I had seen, and was shown that it would be caused by the straight testimony called forth by

the counsel of the True Witness to the Laodiceans. This will have its effect upon the heart of the receiver, and will lead him to exalt the standard and pour forth the straight truth. Some will not bear this straight testimony. They will rise up against it, and this will cause a shaking among God's people.

The testimony of the True Witness has not been half heeded. The solemn testimony upon which the destiny of the church hangs has been lightly esteemed, if not entirely disregarded. This testimony must work deep repentance, and all that truly receive it will obey it and be purified.[14]

Why do I believe in the Spirit of Prophecy? I grew up in a home where this magnificent gift was held in great respect. My father, Elder Neal C. Wilson, always spoke positively and passionately about it. When I was a freshman at La Sierra College, my father sent me a letter in which he quoted a passage from *Steps to Christ*. I treasure that passage. And my mother gave unflinching loyalty to God's Word and the Spirit of Prophecy. I never heard either of my parents disparage the Spirit of Prophecy. My wife also has demonstrated her belief in the Spirit of Prophecy through reading it daily and applying its counsels in our home life.

In my own experience, I have advanced from the initial trust instilled in my heart by my parents to my own deep appreciation of the counsels and clarifications that the Spirit of Prophecy offers us. Whenever I read the Spirit of Prophecy, I see evidence that it was inspired by God—that it is the testimony of Jesus. The Spirit of Prophecy is a great blessing to my life and work.

Why do I believe in the Spirit of Prophecy? In about 1870, a Scottish Presbyterian named William immigrated to the United States from Ireland. He and his wife, Isabella, also from Ireland, lived for some time in Philadelphia, where he worked as an engineer manufacturing locomotives. After a while, though, William and Isabella headed west, to the big tree area of northern California, where William worked in the logging industry. Eventually, he and Isabella settled near Healdsburg, and he became an orchardist and cattle rancher, and he opened a country store as well.

In 1905, William heard that several tents had been pitched north of the Russian River near Healdsburg. Apparently at first William thought the circus had come to town and intended to take his four boys there, thinking that they would enjoy it. Then he learned that it was a Seventh-day Adventist camp meeting. Isabella, who had already become an Adventist, invited him to attend the meetings, and he agreed to go. Ellen White was the preacher. She preached about sinners' need of a Savior and about Christ's power to change lives. At the end of her sermon, Ellen White invited the congregation to accept Jesus as their Savior, and, much to Isabella's surprise, William, who wasn't a particularly religious person, gave his heart to the Lord. He studied this precious Advent message for a year and then decided to close his store on the Sabbath and trust God for the future. When his study convinced him of the biblical basis of the rest of the doctrines that the Seventh-day Adventist Church held, he joined it through baptism. Eventually, he became the first elder of the Healdsburg Seventh-day Adventist Church, and he became known as a generous man who helped people in need.

William and Isabella Wilson were my great-grandparents. My grandfather remembered Ellen White coming to their ranch home when he was a boy and telling stories to him and his brothers as they sat at her feet. The Wilson family owes its knowledge of this precious Advent message to the direct, practical, evangelistic work that Ellen White did. The writings of the Spirit of Prophecy, helpful as they are, take on an even more personal value because of her witness.

# Our responsibility

It is the responsibility of all Seventh-day Adventists—lay members as well as pastors and teachers—to foster belief in and preparation for the Second Coming. Ellen White encourages us with the following thought:

> The return of Christ to our world will not be long delayed. Let this be the keynote of every message.
> The restraining Spirit of God is even now being withdrawn from

the world. Hurricanes, storms, tempests, fire and flood, disasters by sea and land, follow each other in quick succession. . . .

Satan hopes to involve the remnant people of God in the general ruin that is coming upon the earth. As the coming of Christ draws nigh, he will be more determined and decisive in his efforts to overthrow them. . . .

Just before us is the closing struggle of the great controversy when, with "all power and signs and lying wonders, and with all deceivableness of unrighteousness," Satan is to work to misrepresent the character of God, that he may "seduce, if it were possible, even the elect." If there was ever a people in need of constantly increasing light from heaven, it is the people that, in this time of peril, God has called to be the depositaries of His holy law and to vindicate His character before the world. Those to whom has been committed a trust so sacred must be spiritualized, elevated, vitalized, by the truth they profess to believe.[15]

The Spirit of Prophecy calls us each to commit ourselves unreservedly to the proclamation of this precious Advent truth—the three angels' messages, which point people to Christ and His righteousness and the true worship of God. It reminds us that God does have a church today— one that fits the specifications He laid out in Revelation 12:17, of a people who keep the commandments of God and have the testimony of Jesus, which is the magnificent gift of the Spirit of Prophecy. God will guide us and protect us as we carry out the assignment He has given us. The One who inspired the Word of God and the Spirit of Prophecy will not leave us nor forsake us. He will stand by us.

God has commissioned us to preach the same message that Paul preached—Christ crucified, risen, and coming again. We're to preach it in whatever setting we find ourselves. As we do, we have the assurance that He will stand by us forever. He'll never leave us. He'll always be there to give us the encouragement and the understanding we'll need as we face the greatest test that God's people have ever faced throughout the entire great controversy.

One day soon we'll see a small cloud about half the size of a man's hand in the eastern sky. The cloud will grow bigger and bigger and brighter and brighter until it fills the whole sky. Then we'll see that it's made up of all the angels in heaven. They've come to witness what they know will be the greatest event ever to happen on earth—in fact, in the whole universe. And there, seated in the center of the cloud of angels, is our Lord and Savior—the One who came to this earth, lived a perfect life, died on the cross in our place, rose again, and ascended into heaven to become our High Priest. At this very moment He's interceding on our behalf in the Most Holy Place of the sanctuary in heaven. But when He returns to claim us as His own, He'll take off the priestly robes He's wearing now and put on His kingly robes.

When He comes, we'll look up and say, "This is our God for whom we have waited. He will save us." And Christ will look down from the clouds and say, "Well done, good and faithful servants! Enter into the joy of your Lord." What a wonderful time that will be! The difficulties and pain of this life will vanish from our memory as we spend eternity with our Lord.

In preparation for that day, we must commit ourselves, through God's grace and power, to walk with Christ continually, to spend time in His Word, to use the power of prayer, and to enrich our spiritual life by reading daily the writings of the Spirit of Prophecy.

We're almost home. What a shame it would be if we didn't remain faithful to the end because we ignored the guidance for these last days that God has graciously given us through the Spirit of Prophecy.

---

1. White, *Selected Messages*, 2:78.

2. Ibid., 1:41.

3. Ibid.

4. Ellen G. White, *Testimonies for the Church* (Oakland, CA: Pacific Press®, 1900), 6:352.

5. Originally published in the *Journal of the Adventist Theological Society* 8, nos. 1–2 (1997): 19–27, a slightly revised version is available online as Gerhard Pfandl, "The Remnant Church," at http://www.atsjats.org/publication_file.php?pub_id=256&journal=1&type=pdf. This quotation is found on page 3 of the online version; page 220 of the print version.

6. Ibid., page 4 of the online version; page 221 of the print version.

7. Juan Carlos Viera, "God's Guiding Gift," *Adventist Review*, July 24, 1997, 12–15.

8. Ellen G. White, *Testimonies for the Church* (Oakland, CA: Pacific Press®, 1885), 4:390, 391.

9. Ellen G. White, *The Adventist Home* (Nashville: Southern Publishing Association, 1952), 479.

10. Ellen G. White, *Testimonies for the Church* (Mountain View, CA: Pacific Press®, 1909), 9:19.

11. White, *Selected Messages*, 1:48.

12. Ellen G. White, *Testimonies for the Church* (Mountain View, CA: Pacific Press®, 1904), 8:298.

13. Ellen G. White, *In Heavenly Places* (Washington, DC: Review and Herald®, 1967), 127.

14. White, *Testimonies*, 1:179–181.

15. Ellen G. White, *Counsels for the Church* (Boise, ID: Pacific Press®, 1991), 343–345.

# CHAPTER 4

# Our Only Hope

Events taking place around us today are fast fulfilling the prophecies in Daniel, Matthew, and Revelation. Everything seems to be shaking. Political problems are evident all over the world. Moral and cultural decay is rampant. The economies of the world are a hairbreadth away from collapse. Natural disasters are increasingly horrific. Ecumenical movements underway are poised to neutralize the Word of God. They're practically shouting that we're speeding toward the close of this earth's history.

Some people may say, "Oh, these things are all just part of the cycle that goes on and on."

You can believe that if you wish, but I believe these events are signs that Jesus is coming soon. Seventh-day Adventists should never predict the day or the hour, but we have been given the warnings in Scripture that tell us it will happen soon.

What a day to be alive! What a time to be members of God's remnant church and to proclaim the three angels' messages of Revelation 14:6–12! What a time to plead with the Lord for revival, reformation, and the latter rain of the Holy Spirit, which will light this earth with biblical truth, the gospel message of salvation in Christ, and the proclamation of a soon-coming Savior! We're almost home.

The call for revival and reformation is not something that the 2010 Annual Council invented. No committee can commission these spiritual events and then cross them off a checklist and pronounce them completed.

We can't produce revival and reformation—only the Holy Spirit can.

Our call for revival and reformation is not some legalistic, "pull ourselves up by our own bootstraps" initiative. It is centered in Christ and Him alone. He calls us to accept His righteousness and to be empowered by the Holy Spirit to accomplish the last great work before Christ's return—that of proclaiming Christ, His righteousness, and His soon coming. Passages throughout the Bible bring this call to us—passages such as Hosea 6, Joel 2, and the entire book of Acts.

Second Chronicles 7:14 calls us to complete commitment as preparation for fulfilling our role. God says, "If My people who are called by My name will humble themselves, and pray and seek My face, and turn from their wicked ways, then I will hear from heaven, and will forgive their sin and heal their land." We are to humble ourselves before Christ, realizing that our only hope is in Him and His righteousness. Ellen White adds impetus, too, as she looks to the times in which we live. She wrote, "A revival of true godliness among us is the greatest and most urgent of all our needs. To seek this should be our first work."[1]

When we admit our need of revival and reformation in these last days of earth's history, we must then recognize that these experiences must be founded on a full acceptance of Christ and His all-encompassing righteousness. Seventh-day Adventists should be the foremost proclaimers of salvation through Christ and Him alone. He provides the righteousness we need, and that righteousness comes through both justification and sanctification. These two great forms of righteousness cannot be separated. They comprise Christ's all-encompassing righteousness, and they come together or not at all.

## Confusion about righteousness

For various reasons and at various times, people have found the nature and roles of justification and sanctification confusing. Debates about them have created rifts in churches and between members. Some people emphasize justification to the exclusion of sanctification and end up with promoting "cheap grace." Others focus almost exclusively on sanctification and arrive at perfectionism—a form of salvation by works. God's all-encompassing righteousness includes both justification and sanctification. We didn't devise the plan of salvation; He did. It is His way of bringing us into a relationship with Him that begins now and will last forever.

God's plan of salvation is marvelous and assuring and yet incomprehensible in every detail. It is so simple that a child can understand it, yet so grand that we will be studying it throughout eternity. Here are the basics: Jesus, the Son of God, descended to this earth to become one of us, creatures whom He created and who belong to Him. He lived a perfect, sinless life on this earth, died on our behalf, rose to life, intercedes for us in the Most Holy Place of the heavenly sanctuary now, and will soon return to take us to His home.

Yes, Jesus is coming again—and soon. He's coming to take us home. Bible prophecies tell us the "signs" that are to indicate that the time of His return is approaching—political problems around the world, social and moral decay, a fragile economic situation, subtle ecumenical movements, an increase in the number and intensity of natural disasters, and religious confusion—and we see that those signs are present in the world around us today.

God has entrusted to His last-day people the marvelous privilege of proclaiming the messages of the three angels of Revelation 14, which point people to Christ and His righteousness and the true worship of God. He wants us to proclaim His all-encompassing righteousness and to advocate the true worship of God, our Creator, giving glory to Him and proclaiming that His judgment has come. We are to warn that Babylon has fallen and that it is promoting spiritual confusion, and we are to call people to return to a pure and simple understanding of God's plan of salvation. We are to warn against worshiping the beast or his image and receiving the mark of the beast in one's forehead or hand. We must tell people that to receive that mark is to signify that one has accorded the beast, the antichrist, the authority to change God's law and to reject biblical truth and Christ's all-encompassing righteousness.

Seventh-day Adventists have been called to proclaim the truth as it is in Jesus. He and He alone is our salvation. Paul declares unequivocally,

By grace you have been saved through faith, and that not of yourselves; it is the gift of God, not of works, lest anyone should boast. For we are His workmanship, created in Christ Jesus for good works, which God prepared beforehand that we should walk in them (Ephesians 2:8–10).

Make no mistake about it, because Jesus is full of grace, He has made a way of escape for us by providing the plan of salvation through which He justifies us and then sanctifies us. Both justification and sanctification are part of His all-encompassing righteousness. It is His power that accomplishes this in us. As we accept the justification He offers, the robe of righteousness that makes us perfect in the eyes of God, we immediately receive also the power that comes with that justification—Christ's life-changing power of sanctification that makes us more and more like Him.

The righteousness we receive from Christ is all-encompassing. Note, for instance, that Paul first describes the incredible humility of Christ in coming to die as a perfect substitute for us sinners and then speaks of obedience and God's work in and through us:

Therefore, my beloved, as you have always obeyed, not as in my presence only, but now much more in my absence, work out your own salvation with fear and trembling; for it is God who works in you both to will and to do for His good pleasure (Philippians 2:12, 13).

This is not a call for salvation by works. This is a direct call for righteousness by faith in God, "who works in you both to will and to do." It tells us to focus on our relationship to Christ and allow His justifying and sanctifying power to bring us into a right relationship with Him so we can spend eternity with Him.

When we accept Jesus into our lives, He does something mirac-ulous—He changes us into His likeness. He brings about a miraculous, Spirit-filled conversion. Only God can do that. He justifies us, and He allows us to connect with Him so that we become more and more like Him. That's why drunkards become sober. That's why loose-living people become moral. That's why mean-spirited individuals become peacemakers. That's why liars become honest. That's why filthy-minded people become pure. That's why evolutionists become creationists. That's why selfish, self-centered people become selfless, generous benefactors. That's why the unconverted become converted. It's all due to the power of God. He changes our lives, and we begin to produce the fruit of the Spirit. As James declares, "Faith by itself, if it does not have works, is dead" (James 2:17). When we focus our attention entirely on our relationship with Christ, we are placed in a right relationship with Him. What He does in us is done only through His power as we submit to His authority and love.

## A fantastic verse

One of the most fantastic verses in the Bible, 2 Corinthians 5:21, pictures this right relationship. Paul writes, "He made Him who knew no sin to be sin for us, that we might become the righteousness of God in Him." God the Father provided His perfect Son, Christ, as a sacrifice for our sins so that we could receive the perfect righteousness of Christ. What an incredible plan of salvation! No wonder we will be studying it throughout eternity! No wonder when we get to heaven we'll take off our crowns and throw them at Jesus' feet in overwhelming gratitude and love for His power to save! No wonder we will sing His praises then and throughout eternity! No wonder we'll proclaim God's unbelievable love by singing

> Amazing grace! how sweet the sound,
> That saved a wretch like me!
> I once was lost, but now am found,
> Was blind but now I see.

This is the "born again" experience Jesus was speaking of when He told Nicodemus, "Most assuredly, I say to you, unless one is born again, he cannot see the kingdom of God" (John 3:3).

This born-again experience, which comes entirely through Christ's power, puts us in the right relationship with Him, and makes us into new people. Second Corinthians 5:17 states, "If anyone is in Christ, he is a new creation: old things have passed away; behold, all things have become new." As the Holy Spirit leads us to confess our sins and fall at the foot of the cross before Christ, we become new creatures and are cleansed of our sins. John declares, "If we confess our sins, He is faithful and just to forgive us our sins and to cleanse us from all unrighteousness" (1 John 1:9). John also declares, "As many as received Him, to them He gave the right to become children of God, to those who believe in His name: who were born, not of blood, nor of the will of the flesh, nor of the will of man, but of God" (John 1:12, 13). Furthermore, the beloved disciple writes, "Whatever is born of God overcomes the world. And this is the victory that has overcome the world—our faith" (1 John 5:4).

These verses speak of God's all-encompassing righteousness, through which we are saved by grace and we live by faith—all provided through Christ Jesus our Savior and Lord! That is why we can join Paul in proclaiming,

I have been crucified with Christ; it is no longer I who live, but Christ lives in me; and the life which I now live in the flesh I live by faith in the Son of God, who loved me and gave Himself for me (Galatians 2:20).

Ultimately, Paul sums it all up in this simple statement: "For to me, to live is Christ" (Philippians 1:21).

Paul gave a remarkable explanation of God's all-encompassing righteousness to Titus, a convert from paganism. When Titus was a young pastor, Paul put him in charge of a parish on the island of Crete. This large island that lies south of Greece in the Mediterranean Sea had centuries before been the center of the powerful Minoan civilization, which had rivaled those of Mesopotamia and Egypt. In Paul's day, the Cretans were pagans. They were influenced by half-converted Jews, who emphasized myths and laws. Crete was a crossroads of trade and had many visitors, so it isn't surprising that strong disagreements erupted occasionally.

Paul wrote a letter to Titus counseling him and the Cretans regarding practical Christian living. Of course, Paul was instructing us as well as the Cretans when he wrote,

> The grace of God that brings salvation has appeared to all men, teaching us that, denying ungodliness and worldly lusts, we should live soberly, righteously, and godly in the present age, looking for the blessed hope and glorious appearing of our great God and Savior Jesus Christ (Titus 2:11–13).

Oh, I am anxiously anticipating that "blessed hope and glorious appearing" of Christ, aren't you! Not long ago, I lost my precious father. He was a strong church leader, a wonderful father, and one of my best friends. Because of Christ's grace and power, I will see my father again. Praise God, we're almost home!

In Titus 3, Paul instructs the young pastor to remind his parishioners

> to be subject to rulers and authorities, to obey, to be ready for every good work, to speak evil of no one, to be peaceable, gentle, showing all humility to all men. For we ourselves were also once foolish, disobedient, deceived, serving various lusts and pleasures, living in malice and envy, hateful and hating one another (Titus 3:1–3).

Paul has listed our problems. Now notice what he says about how we changed. He begins by reminding us of "the kindness and the love of God our Savior toward man" (verse 4). Then, in verses 5 and 6, Paul indicates that it was "not by works of righteousness which we have done, but according to His mercy He saved us, through the washing of regeneration and the renewing of the Holy Spirit." Paul shows that we are justified through Christ's power: "According to His mercy He saved us, through the washing of regeneration," and we are sanctified through Christ's power too—through the "renewing of the Holy Spirit whom He poured out on us abundantly through Jesus Christ our Savior."

Paul goes on to say that "having been justified by His grace we . . . become heirs according to the hope of eternal life" (verse 7). So, we are justified by Christ—covered with His robe of righteousness, which is imputed to us, making us appear perfect before the Father, just as if we had not sinned. It is Christ's righteousness that accomplishes this.

Then, in verse 8, Paul says, "This is a faithful saying, and these things I want you to affirm constantly, that those who have believed in God should be careful to maintain good works. These things are good and profitable to men." The good works that Paul mentions here are a result of the sanctifying power of Christ. The Holy Spirit works in us to make us become more and more like Christ. We are totally dependent on our relationship with Christ for sanctification. This, too, is Christ's righteousness.

## A biblical truth

The Spirit of Prophecy seconds the biblical truth of Christ's all-encompassing righteousness, giving us some wonderful insights into it. In the next several paragraphs I share some encouraging and helpful statements that come from the marvelous little book *Steps to Christ*.[2] Two very helpful passages are found on pages 62 and 63, and pages 70 and 71.

The condition of eternal life is now just what it always has been,—just what it was in Paradise before the fall of our first parents,—perfect obedience to the law of God, perfect righteousness. If eternal life were granted on any condition short of this, then the happiness of the whole universe would be imperiled. The way would be open for sin, with all its train of woe and misery, to be immortalized.

It was possible for Adam, before the fall, to form a righteous character by obedience to God's law. But he failed to do this, and because of his sin our natures are fallen, and we cannot make ourselves righteous. Since we are sinful, unholy, we cannot perfectly obey the holy law. We have no righteousness of our own with which to meet the claims of the law of God. But Christ has made a way of escape for us. He lived on earth amid trials and temptations such as we have to meet. He lived a sinless life. He died for us, and now He offers to take our sins and give us His righteousness. If you give yourself to Him, and accept Him as your Saviour, then, sinful as your life may have been, for His sake you are accounted righteous. Christ's character stands in place of your character, and you are accepted before God just as if you had not sinned.

More than this, Christ changes the heart. He abides in your heart by faith. You are to maintain this connection with Christ by faith and the continual surrender of your will to Him; and so long as you do this, He will work in you to will and to do according to His good pleasure. So you may say, "The life which I now live in the flesh I live by the faith of the Son of God who loved me, and gave Himself for me." So Jesus said to His disciples, "It is not ye that speak, but the Spirit of your Father which speaketh in you." Then with Christ working in you, you will manifest the same spirit and do the same good works,—works of righteousness, obedience.

So we have nothing in ourselves of which to boast. We have no ground for self-exaltation. Our only ground of hope is in the righteousness of Christ imputed to us, and in that wrought by His Spirit working in and through us.

By *faith* you became Christ's, and by faith you are to grow up in Him,—by giving and taking. You are to *give* all,—your heart, your will, your service,—give yourself to Him to obey all His requirements; and you must *take* all,—Christ, the fullness of all blessing, to abide in your heart, to be your strength, your righteousness, your everlasting helper,—to give you power to obey.

Consecrate yourself to God in the morning; make this your very first work. Let your prayer be, "Take me, O Lord, as wholly Thine. I lay all my plans at Thy feet. Use me today in Thy service. Abide with me, and let all my work be wrought in Thee." This is a daily matter. Each morning consecrate yourself to God for that day. Surrender all your plans to Him, to be carried out or given up as His providence shall indicate. Thus day by day you may be giving your life into the hands of God, and thus your life will be molded more and more after the life of Christ.

A life in Christ is a life of restfulness. There may be no ecstasy of feeling, but there should be an abiding, peaceful trust. Your hope is not in yourself; it is in Christ. Your weakness is united to His strength, your ignorance to His wisdom, your frailty to His enduring might. So you are not to look to yourself, not to let the mind dwell upon self, but look to Christ. Let the mind dwell upon His love, upon the beauty, the perfection of His character. Christ in His self-denial, Christ in His humiliation, Christ in His purity and holiness. Christ in His matchless love,—this is the subject for the soul's contemplation. It is by loving Him, copying Him, depending wholly upon Him, that you are to be transformed into His likeness.

No wonder Paul proclaims,

Seeing then that we have a great high priest who has passed through the heavens, Jesus the Son of God, let us hold fast our confession. For we do not have a high priest who cannot sympathize with our weaknesses, but was in all points tempted as we are, yet without sin. Let us therefore come boldly to the throne of grace, that we may obtain mercy and find grace to help in time of need (Hebrews 4:14–16).

What a wonderful Savior—He came to this earth to take our place and to provide a way of escape for us! What love and humility Christ demonstrated in coming to die for us! Ellen White wrote,

It would have been almost infinite humiliation for the Son of God to take man's nature, even when Adam stood in his innocence in Eden. But Jesus accepted humanity when the race had been weakened by four thousand years of sin. Like every child of Adam He accepted the results of the working of the great law of heredity. What these results were is shown in the history of His earthly ancestors. He came with such a heredity to share our sorrows and temptations, and to give us the example of a sinless life.[3]

# Our all in all

Christ is our all in all. He has provided salvation for us through His all-encompassing righteousness. We are to depend totally and completely on Him and His righteousness and to look to Him. Ellen White indicates that

in taking upon Himself man's nature in its fallen condition, Christ did not in the least participate in its sin. . . .

We should have no misgivings in regard to the perfect sinlessness of the human nature of Christ. Our faith must be an intelligent faith, looking unto Jesus in perfect confidence, in full and entire faith in the atoning Sacrifice. . . . Divine power is placed upon man, that he may become a partaker of the divine nature, having escaped the corruption that is in the world through lust. This is why repenting, believing man can be made the righteousness of God in Christ.[4]

Let us never claim any righteousness of our own. Let us always look to Jesus. We cannot work our way to heaven by our own efforts or self-righteousness. Our salvation comes entirely from Christ and His all-encompassing righteousness.

Ellen White described the righteousness we receive from Christ in her book *The Desire of Ages*:

The righteousness which Christ taught is conformity of heart and life to the revealed will of God. Sinful men can become righteous only as they have faith in God and maintain a vital connection with Him. Then true godliness will elevate the thoughts and ennoble the life. Then the external forms of religion accord with the Christian's internal purity.[5]

We are not to think that we are righteous in our own right or that we can improve ourselves through our own efforts. We are completely dependent on Christ for any changes in our lives as we submit to Him. Let us never boast of being perfect or having attained perfection. Notice what Ellen White says in that wonderful new compilation titled *True Revival*:

No one who claims holiness is really holy. Those who are registered as holy in the books of Heaven are not aware of the fact, and are the last ones to boast of their own goodness. None of the prophets and apostles ever professed holiness, not even Daniel, Paul, or John. The righteous never make such a claim.

The more nearly they resemble Christ, the more they lament their unlikeness to Him; for their consciences are sensitive, and they regard sin more as God regards it. They have exalted views of God and of the great plan of salvation; and their hearts, humbled under a sense of their own unworthiness, are alive to the honor of being accounted members of the royal family, sons and daughters of the King Eternal.[6]

Let no one in the Seventh-day Adventist Church think of himself or herself as better than anyone else. Let no one accuse others of not being holy or perfect. We are all sinners standing at the foot of the cross in need of a Savior who provides for us His all-encompassing righteousness, which brings us both justification and sanctification. We owe everything to Jesus.

This spiritual relation can be established only by the exercise of the personal faith. This faith must express on our part supreme preference, perfect reliance, entire consecration. Our will must be wholly yielded to the divine will, our feelings, desires, interests, and honor identified with the prosperity of Christ's kingdom and the honor of His cause, we constantly receiving grace from Him, and Christ accepting gratitude from us.[7]

We must not examine each other, looking for the other's sins and thinking that we are better than those other sinners. We are not to bring about confusion and division within the church with accusations that others are more sinful. We are not to think of ourselves as perfect except as Christ's justifying and sanctifying righteousness covers our imperfections. Our salvation comes entirely through the righteousness of Christ—we bring no righteousness of our own. Since we all stand upon level ground, we all are entirely dependent upon Christ and His righteousness for our standing with God, for our salvation; we all are to be unified in word and action.

Ellen White tells us,

> The secret of unity is found in the quality of believers in Christ. The reason for all division, discord, and difference is found in separation from Christ. Christ is the center to which all should be attracted; for the nearer we approach the center, the closer we shall come together in feeling, in sympathy, in love, growing into the character and image of Jesus.[8]

This is the secret of our preparation for heaven, for living where sin doesn't despoil our homes and relationships: Christ's all-encompassing righteousness. We're almost home. We need to be preparing to live there. We need to be seeing more and more of Jesus.

---

1. White, *Selected Messages*, 1:121.
2. Ellen G. White, *Steps to Christ* (Washington, DC: Reveiw and Herald®, 1956).
3. Ellen G. White, *The Desire of Ages* (Mountain View, CA: Pacific Press®, 1898), 49.
4. White, *Selected Messages*, 1:256.
5. White, *The Desire of Ages*, 310.
6. Ellen G. White, *True Revival* (Hagerstown, MD: Review and Herald®, 2010), 62, 63.
7. Ibid., 50, 51.
8. White, *Selected Messages*, 1:259.

# CHAPTER 5

# Good News About the Judgment

As Seventh-day Adventists, we have long understood our unique mission, and, in fact, our very character, to spring from Revelation 14:6–12, the three angels' messages. We can't satisfactorily fulfill the mission God has given us if we don't understand this passage. Seventh-day Adventist theology and mission are inseparable. We are to preach and teach and live the precious three angels' messages.

Each of these angels has a special message. The first one directs people back to the true worship of God. The second announces that apostate religious organizations have turned from Bible truth and are fallen. And the third reveals the mark that distinguishes those who oppose God from those who serve Him. God's people will worship on the seventh-day Sabbath and treat it as a holy day. This regard for the day God calls His is the "sign" that these people are His too. Conversely, attempting to substitute any other day of the week in place of the seventh-day Sabbath is the mark of the beast—the mark identifying those who disregard God and His will.

In some places these days, people may say the messages these angels brought are politically incorrect and not advisable to preach in public. But these are the messages God has asked us to publicize. They are the most important messages we can preach. They are our theology and our mission! These messages constitute the reason people become Seventh-day Adventists, members of this wonderful remnant church.

In this chapter, I will focus on the first angel's message, which speaks of God's creatorship, the judgment, and the sanctuary message—all of which constitute the theology and the mission God has given us to share, and consequently, all of which are subjects close to the hearts of Seventh-day Adventists, subjects that we must preach and teach!

Revelation 14:6, 7, the passage that contains the first angel's message, says,

> And I saw another angel fly in the midst of heaven, having the everlasting gospel to preach unto them that dwell on the earth, and to every nation, and kindred, and tongue, and people, saying with a loud voice, Fear God, and give glory to him: for the hour of his judgment is come: and worship him that made heaven, and earth, and the sea, and the fountains of waters.

Verse 6 speaks of "another angel." There are many angels, or messengers, in Revelation. This is the first of the three special angels pictured in chapter 14. This angel is carrying the most magnificent news: the "everlasting gospel"—the plan of salvation, the good news that Christ paid our debt, has borne our punishment on the cross, and now He is interceding on our behalf as our High Priest.

Verse 6 also refers to "the everlasting gospel." That everlasting gospel is the good news that we obtain righteousness through having faith in Christ. He offers imputed righteousness through justification, and imparted righteousness through sanctification, and ultimately glorification—all through Christ. We are to take this message of Christ's righteousness and the salvation given freely to all who believe throughout the entire world—to every nation, every people group, every language group.

Verse 7 tells us that the angel delivers the message "with a loud voice." That tells us we're not to whisper this precious message. We're to tell it with a loud voice. We're to tell people to "fear"—or, in other words, to *respect* and *honor*—God; to "give glory to him," not to themselves, because the time of His judgment has come. We're to give glory to Him by showing our loyalty to Him through trusting Him to supply all our needs—including our need for righteousness.

We're to give glory to Him in the way we live, our lifestyle; in the way we use our time; in how we dress; in our daily choices; in what we eat. Believe me, what we eat and drink directly affects our spiritual life. The Bible and the Spirit of Prophecy tell us this. So, we're to abstain from harmful substances like alcohol, tobacco, caffeine, and drugs and live a balanced, temperate life under the Holy Spirit's direction. We're to give glory to Him because the time of judgment and salvation is here.

This special announcement, the message of the first angel, helps turn people back to the true worship of God—the One who made heaven, the earth, the sea, and . . . everything. He is the Creator. He is worthy of our praise and worship because He created us. That's why we worship Him on the seventh day, the Sabbath. We do so because He asked us to and because the Sabbath is a memorial of His creatorship. This precious message of a recent creation in six literal, consecutive, twenty-four-hour days is the basis of our worship on this sacred day, the Sabbath— the same kind of Sabbath God created six thousand years ago. This precious biblical truth of a literal creation has come under fierce attack by unbelieving secularists and humanists and is even being attacked or dismissed by some Seventh-day Adventists.

Our church has long held to the historical-biblical method of interpreting Scripture—untangling difficult passages by looking to other parts of Scripture for clues, thus allowing the Bible to interpret itself, line upon line, precept upon precept. One of the most sinister attacks against the Bible and Creation is made by those who believe in the historical-*critical* method of interpreting the Bible, which is a deadly enemy of our theology and mission. This approach gives more credence to scholars than to the plain statements of Scripture. The critics believe their education and intellectual resources give the insight that enables them to judge what parts of Scripture are true and what parts aren't. Stay away from this type of approach; it doesn't lead people to trust God and His Word and will, in fact, corrupt an organization's theology and mission.

If we didn't take the description of Creation in Genesis 1 and 2 literally, there'd be no reason to worship God on the literal seventh day of a literal seven-day week. The first angel's message is a clarion call to everyone in the world to worship God, the Creator, on the true Sabbath, the seventh day.

Other important parts of the first angel's message are the "everlasting gospel" and the "judgment" message. In fact, the primary theme of the first angel's message is the judgment of all who have ever lived. This judgment is taking place in heaven right now. It is a part of the plan of salvation that God formulated before the foundation of this world—a plan based upon Christ's work on this earth and in the sanctuary in heaven to provide salvation for us.

## The earthly sanctuary

When the children of Israel left Egypt and were wandering in the Sinai Desert, God assigned Moses to construct an earthly sanctuary. The services conducted in that sanctuary would remind the world of Christ's death on the cross for our sins and the ultimate transference of sin to the one who deserves to bear it—Satan. Through the earthly sanctuary service, God taught the world how Christ would handle the sin problem and conduct the judgment.

Moses recorded God's initiation of the project in Exodus 25:8, 9. God said, "Let them make me a sanctuary; that I may dwell among them. According to all that I shew thee, after the pattern of the tabernacle, and the pattern of all the instruments thereof, even so shall ye make it."

For the most part, the earthly sanctuary and its services taught us about Christ's righteousness and how the judgment was to be carried out. Hebrews 8:2 says that Jesus is "a minister of the sanctuary, and of the true tabernacle, which the Lord pitched, and not man." And Hebrews 8:5 indicates that the earthly sanctuary was a "shadow of heavenly things."

The sanctuary shows the world how God is working to save us. It is a key doctrine of Seventh-day Adventists. You can read the descriptions of the sanctuary furniture and structure in Exodus 25:2–8, and you'll also find beautiful descriptions in chapter 30 of *Patriarchs and Prophets*.

Reflect briefly on some amazing facts about the sanctuary:

- The earthly sanctuary was built using the best materials that the children of Israel could provide. Since it had to be portable, though it was impressive, it had to be compact—fifty-five feet long by fifteen feet wide and high. The walls of the building were made of boards overlaid with gold and set in silver sockets.
- The "walls" of the courtyard in which the sanctuary building stood were made of fine linen. The sacrifices were burned on the brazen altar that stood in the courtyard in front of the sanctuary, and the atoning blood from the sacrifices, which represented Christ's blood that was shed for us, was sprinkled on the horns of that altar.
- The laver where the priests washed represented the cleansing power of Christ.
- The showbread, which was stacked on a golden table in the Holy Place of the sanctuary, represented Jesus, who is the Bread of Life for each of us.
- The seven-branched candlestick (actually, lampstand), which was made from one piece of gold, represented Jesus the Light of the world and of our lives.
- The golden altar of incense, representing God's presence with a fire that He kindled, stood before the curtain separating the Holy Place from the Most Holy Place. The smoke that ascended from that altar represented the worshipers' prayers and petitions to God for forgiveness. The horns of that altar were touched with blood from the sin offering, and the blood of the sacrifice sprinkled before the veil showed the transfer of guilt from the person to the sanctuary.
- The curtain between the Holy Place and the Most Holy Place didn't reach the ceiling, so the smoke of the incense offered in the Holy Place drifted into the Most Holy Place and over the mercy seat on the ark of the covenant, where the symbolic service of atonement and intercession took place, connecting heaven and earth.
- The ark of the covenant was made of acacia wood overlaid with gold. It contained the Ten Commandments inscribed in stone by God

Himself and some manna and Aaron's rod that budded, showing God's constant interest in our lives and His care for our needs. The ark's mercy seat was cast as a single piece of solid gold. Two golden cherubim stood over it, each with one wing stretched on high and the other folded in reverence and humility. This represented the reverence with which heaven regards the law of God and the interest of heavenly beings in the plan of redemption: what the judgment is all about, our deliverance through the blood of Jesus, our humble submission and confession to Him of our recognition of our need of forgiveness and of the deliverance that He offers.

- Above the mercy seat, the Shekinah glory gave a visible manifestation of God's presence. The holiness of the sanctuary and God's presence and power were awe-inspiring. And He is just as surely with us today as we worship in His house as He was with ancient Israel as they worshiped in their sanctuary. He is here with us today through the Holy Spirit; that's why it's so important that we are reverent when we're in His sanctuary.

Of the sanctuary services of ancient Israel, Ellen White wrote, "In the work of Christ for our redemption, symbolized by the sanctuary service, 'mercy and truth are met together; righteousness and peace have kissed each other.' Psalm 85:10."[1] All of those services demonstrated God's plan of redemption through the blood of Christ.

Typically, a sinner would come to the door of the tabernacle, place his hand on the sacrificial animal's head, and confess his sin, thus symbolically transferring the sin from himself to the innocent sacrifice. Then, by his own hand he would kill the sacrifice. Normally, the blood was then sprinkled by the priest before the veil in the Holy Place, showing the transference of the sin to the sanctuary.

This spiritual work went on day after day. Can you imagine the build-up of tangible blood and of intangible—but nonetheless real—sins in the Holy Place? Thus it became necessary to remove the sins. So God commanded that atonement be made for each of the holy apartments.

Once a year, the high priest entered the Most Holy Place to cleanse the entire sanctuary of sin. On that annual Day of Atonement, two goats were brought to the door of the tabernacle. One was slain as a sin offering for the people, with the blood—which represented Christ's blood shed for us—being brought into the Most Holy Place and sprinkled on the mercy seat. Then the high priest would place his hands on the head of the live goat—the scapegoat, which represented Satan— and confess all the accumulated sins of Israel, thus transferring the sins from the sanctuary to the scapegoat. The scapegoat was then led into the wilderness to die, showing that Satan will ultimately bear the final penalty of sin and will die, which will put an end to his temptations.

## On the cross

Now, let's review what happened at Christ's death on the cross on Friday afternoon at the time of the evening sacrifice. The priest at the temple in Jerusalem was about to kill the lamb when Christ died. The curtain separating the Holy Place and Most Holy Place was, as Matthew 27:51 records, "rent in twain from the top to the bottom," and the sacrificial lamb escaped. *The Desire of Ages* says,

> The great sacrifice has been made. . . . A new and living way is prepared for all. No longer need sinful, sorrowing humanity await the coming of the high priest. Henceforth the Saviour was to officiate as priest and advocate in the heaven of heavens.[2]

Jesus, the Sacrifice, became our High Priest.

After Jesus' resurrection, He rose to heaven and began the special ministry of interceding for us as our High Priest. Hebrews 4:14–16 says,

> Seeing then that we have a great high priest, that is passed into the heavens, Jesus the Son of God, let us hold fast our profession. For we have not an high priest which cannot be touched with the feeling of our infirmities; but was in all points tempted like as we are, yet without sin. Let us therefore come boldly unto the

throne of grace, that we may obtain mercy, and find grace to help in time of need.

This was the life-saving result of the cross and the nails.

It is Christ's right and privilege to represent us—to be our High Priest, our Advocate, our Lawyer. *The Great Controversy* indicates that "in the temple in heaven, the dwelling place of God, His throne is established in righteousness and judgment."[3] Hebrews 6:19 indicates that He entered "into that within the veil" in the Holy Place, doing His work of mediation there for eighteen centuries. Then, according to the prophecy of Daniel 8:14, after "two thousand and three hundred days," the sanctuary was to be "cleansed." At that time, Christ entered the Most Holy Place to begin His final work of ministry and then judgment.

We are now living during Christ's final work of sanctuary cleansing—during the judgment. The sanctuary doctrine and the judgment are important theological reasons why Seventh-day Adventists are engaged in mission. Soon Christ will return and force Satan to bear the final penalty. The blood of Jesus Christ, our Sacrifice, shed on the cross, and the ministry of Jesus Christ, our High Priest, carried out in the heavenly sanctuary, have one purpose—that you and I and all who submit to Him, confessing our sins and accepting Him as our Savior, may be made right with God and have eternal life. It's because of Christ's ministry on the cross and in the heavenly sanctuary that eternal life can be ours. We don't have to fear the judgment if we know the Lamb, if we know the High Priest, if we know the coming King.

The three angels' messages change people. The Holy Spirit works on the hearts of those who hear the Advent message. He does this through the preaching and witness of those who love and serve God.

A few years ago, Vasili, a police officer in Moldova, became convicted about Bible truth and this precious message and wanted to be baptized as a Seventh-day Adventist. But when he told his family and friends about his newfound faith, they reacted negatively. His father and mother said they would disown him; his brother said he would no longer consider him to be a brother; his wife said she would divorce him; and his boss, the police commander, said he would never give Vasili Sabbaths off.

Vasili agonized with God about what he should do. He prayed that God would give him a direct answer to his question, proposing that when he opened his Bible God do so by directing him to a text that would tell him what he should do. When Vasili opened his Bible, the first passage that caught his eye was Matthew 10:35–38, where Jesus warns that when we follow Him, the members of our family may become our enemies, and where He goes on to say that those who love father or mother more than Him are not worthy of Him, and then tells us to take up our cross and follow Him.

Vasili thanked God for speaking to him through the Bible, and at his next opportunity, he was baptized. When he told his wife that he had been baptized, she said she had the papers for a divorce filled out and ready to sign. Rather than becoming upset, Vasili told his wife that he loved her and suggested that she go with him to tell his parents. His wife agreed, thinking that his parents would help her persuade him to back out of his commitment. But when they visited his parents, it was obvious that the Holy Spirit had been at work, because rather than becoming upset and yelling at him, they responded positively, and so did his brother.

At this turn of events, Vasili's wife became extremely upset and frustrated. But Vasili remained calm, refusing to argue with her or become angry at her unreasonableness.

Next, Vasili told his commanding police officer that he had been baptized and handed him his resignation. The officer handed the resignation letter back to Vasili and told him to take a week off to think about what he was doing. At the end of the week, Vasili returned and again handed over his resignation. But instead of accepting the resignation, the officer promoted Vasili so he wouldn't have Sabbath problems.

About this time, a serious problem arose that threatened to cause Vasili's wife, a cashier, a lot of trouble. At the end of a day at work, she counted the money in her cash register as usual—and found that she was short. She didn't have the money she should have had. Her boss said she owed the company the difference, which would have hurt Vasili and her financially.

That night she asked Vasili to pray for her, and he did. And the next day she found a bookkeeping error that accounted for the exact amount she was missing. At that, Vasili told her that she should give her heart to God, but she said No.

A while later, the mother of Vasili's wife was given a diagnosis of cancer. That devastated Vasili's wife. Vasili and his wife visited her mother and prayed for her, and through God's intervention, she was healed! That was enough for Vasili's wife. She went straight to the Seventh-day Adventist Church and was baptized!

God works in incredible ways when people accept this marvelous Advent message and stand for Him. But there are thousands who haven't yet heard the truth God has given us to share.

So we must proclaim the first angel's message far and wide by our life and by our words. We must encourage people to "fear God, and give glory to Him; for the hour of His judgment is come: and worship Him that made heaven, and earth, and the sea, and the fountains of waters."

We don't have to fear the judgment if we place ourselves in Christ's saving and ministering hands. We can say with Paul, "Wherefore he is able also to save them to the uttermost that come unto God by him, seeing he ever liveth to make intercession for them" (Hebrews 7:25).

What a message for this last-day Advent movement to carry to the world! This beautiful message—the proclamation of the first, second, and third angels' messages, which call people back to the true and biblical worship of God—will drive our mission.

We're almost home! Let's do what we can to fulfill our mission—to hasten that day when Jesus returns.

---

1. White, *Patriarchs and Prophets*, 349.
2. White, *The Desire of Ages*, 769.
3. Ellen G. White, *The Great Controversy* (Mountain View, CA: Pacific Press©, 1911), 415.

# CHAPTER 6

# How God Defines Success

How do you define success? Is it being given a corner office? Becoming the CEO of a burgeoning company? Having a lake house? Taking Caribbean cruises? Shopping all you want? Owning a Porsche, a BMW, a Lexus, and a few Mercedes? Or being a popular politician or comedian or movie star?

Success meant something different to the apostle Paul. Most people would think his definition was upside down. He told the Corinthians,

If I should want to boast I should certainly be no fool to be proud of my experiences, and I should be speaking nothing but the sober truth. Yet I am not going to do so, for I don't want anyone to think more highly of me than his experience of me and what he hears of me should warrant. So tremendous, however, were the revelations that God gave me that, in order to prevent my becoming absurdly conceited, I was given a physical handicap— one of Satan's angels—to harass me and effectually stop any conceit. Three times I begged the Lord for it to leave me, but His reply has been, "My grace is enough for you: for where there is weakness, My power is shown the more completely." Therefore, I have cheerfully made up my mind to be proud of my weaknesses, because they mean a deeper experience of the power of Christ. I can even enjoy weaknesses, suffering, privations, persecutions and difficulties for Christ's sake. For my very weakness makes me strong in Him (2 Corinthians 12:6–10;* the King James Version says, "When I am weak, then am I strong").

That doesn't sound to me like something people seeking power or praise would say or even think. Glorying in our infirmities? Taking pleasure in persecution and reproaches? It is when I'm weak that I am strong? What is Paul trying to say?

Could it be that he was saying the world's definition of success is based on self-centeredness and pride, while Christ's definition of success means faithfully serving God and our fellow human beings without taking credit for what we do?

Accumulating wealth or the admiration of the people around us may define success in a world in which death is eternal. But those who expect to live forever in a land where there's no pain or death, where there's no need to give priority to self or to compete with others for all that makes life good, have a good reason to view success differently.

So, it makes sense for Paul to counsel the Corinthians, "He that glorieth, let him glory in the Lord. For not he that commendeth himself is approved, but whom the Lord commendeth" (2 Corinthians 10:17, 18, KJV). He also said,

As your spiritual teacher I give this piece of advice to each one of you. Don't cherish exaggerated ideas of yourself or your importance, but try to have a sane estimate of your capabilities by the light of the faith that God has given to you all (Romans 12:3).

The Bible's valuation of the people whose stories it tells certainly indicates that it has a different definition of success than is popular today. Its heroes were people who, at least for much of their lives, would today be judged as anything but successful. There was Noah, for instance, who preached for 120 years without converting anyone other than the members

---

* I generally use the King James Version of the Bible, but I've chosen to use mostly J. B. Phillips's translation in this chapter since that translation conveys Scripture in a very practical way.

of his own family. And Joseph, who so aggravated his brothers that they sold him into slavery—where he later was imprisoned on charges of attempted rape. And Moses, who, driven by his temper, killed a man when he was young and exploded in rage when the people he was leading to freedom lost their confidence in him. And the prophet Elijah, who, after winning a great victory for God on Mount Carmel, ran like a scared rabbit from an angry woman. And Jeremiah, who claimed to be a prophet but whose messages were so bleak that the authorities had him thrown into a miserable, stinking pit. And Mary, whose only Son was charged with being both a heretic and a rebel, tried, and given the death penalty. And Paul, who was rocketing up the path toward leadership in his nation but then turned onto a path that led to repeated arrests and ultimately to his execution.

Why does Scripture praise these characters and count them as being really great, really successful? It does so because they were following God's recipe for success—they humbly submitted themselves to God and lived to fulfill His plan—lived to serve people with love and humility and to bring them to God.

## The ultimate example

Jesus, of course, gave us the ultimate example. He reached the pinnacle of success—living a life of complete submission to His heavenly Father and of full-time service to others. He lived on earth to set an example for us, and He died to free us from sin. We owe everything to Him.

Years ago someone penned these words:

> He was born in an obscure village, the child of a peasant woman. He grew up in another obscure village, where He worked in a carpenter shop until He was thirty. Then for three years He was an itinerant preacher. He never had a family or owned a home. He never set foot inside a big city. He never traveled far from the place where He was born. He never wrote a book or held an office. He did none of the things that usually accompany greatness.
>
> While He was still a young man, the tide of popular opinion

turned against Him. His friends deserted Him. He was turned over to His enemies and went through the mockery of a trial. He was nailed to a cross between two thieves. While He was dying, His executioners gambled for the only piece of property He had—His coat. When He was dead, He was taken down and laid in a borrowed grave.

Nineteen centuries have come and gone, and today He is the central figure for much of the human race. All the armies that ever marched, and all the navies that ever sailed, and all the parliaments that ever sat, and all the kings that ever reigned, put together, have not affected the life of man upon this earth as powerfully as this one solitary life.[1]

Here's how J. B. Phillips translated Paul's brief but powerful summary of what Jesus' incarnation meant to Him and to His Father in heaven:

Let Christ himself be your example as to what your attitude should be. For he, who had always been God by nature, did not cling to his prerogatives as God's equal, but stripped himself of all privilege by consenting to be a slave by nature and being born as mortal man. And, having become man, he humbled himself by living a life of utter obedience, even to the extent of dying, and the death he died was the death of a common criminal. That is why God has now lifted him so high, and has given him the name beyond all names, so that at the name of Jesus "every knee shall bow", whether in Heaven or earth or under the earth. And that is why, in the end, "every tongue shall confess" that Jesus Christ is the Lord, to the glory of God the Father (Philippians 2:5–11).

What a sacrifice! What love for us! What a formula for success! No wonder that every knee will bow to Him. That is true biblical success. That is how to be strong through being weak.

Hanging in the family room of the home of one of my brothers-in-law is a picture of Christ on the cross and a man kneeling in front of Him. There's an inscription on the picture that reads something like this: "Kneeling in faith at the cross, the sinner has reached the highest place to which man can attain."[2] In that beautiful little book *Steps to Christ*, which everyone should make one of their treasured companions, Ellen White urged,

> Let us keep our eyes fixed upon Christ, and He will preserve us. Looking unto Jesus, we are safe. Nothing can pluck us out of His hand. In constantly beholding Him, we "are changed into the same image from glory to glory, even as by the Spirit of the Lord."[3]

We owe everything good that we have and are to Christ, and it is essential that we realize our constant need of Him. Paul put it this way: "We can see that it was while we were powerless to help ourselves that Christ died for sinful men" (Romans 5:6). He died for us.

Whatever our circumstances, we must realize that we can have true success only as we stay connected to Christ. He is the only source of the love, the motivation, and the strength we must have to live lives of humble service to others—which is Heaven's definition of success.

# Real-life examples

We can find many ways to follow Christ by giving ourselves in selfless service for Him and for our fellow human beings—countless ways in which we can become strong by becoming weak, countless ways to deny self and lift Jesus up.

There are many examples of how people living in today's world have been able to do just that. There are countless stories of humble Christian sacrifice and service that no one ever hears. But the Lord knows each one; they are very important to Him and are recorded in heaven's books even if no one here ever hears about them. We reach the pinnacle of success when we do the will of our heavenly Father where we live and work, whether our place of service is in an office, or in some far-off, obscure location, or within the walls of our own home. If we depend upon God, He'll make us truly successful wherever we serve Him through helping others.

In chapter 3 of this book, I mentioned a beautiful spiritual gem from *Steps to Christ* that my father copied into a letter he sent me when I was a college student. Here are the words that so impressed me:

> Consecrate yourself to God in the morning; make this your very first work. Let your prayer be, "Take me, O Lord, as wholly Thine. I lay all my plans at Thy feet. Use me today in Thy service. Abide with me, and let all my work be wrought in Thee." . . . Thus day by day you may be giving your life into the hands of God, and thus your life will be molded more and more after the life of Christ.[4]

We must ask the Holy Spirit to lead us so that we will know how to serve God and those around us with an unselfish love and a complete commitment to Christ's example. You may work as a computer programmer, nurse, auto mechanic, engineer, pastor, business person, teacher, physician, graphic artist, musician, speech pathologist, or in some other occupation. Whatever your work may be, the Lord wants to work through you. He wants you to share Christ and His great Advent message with those who haven't yet accepted Him and the salvation He's offering them. There are people who need to hear what Jesus has done for you. They need to know that Jesus is ministering for us today as our Advocate and High Priest in the Most Holy Place of the heavenly sanctuary.

Christ has done so much for you; what will you do for Him?

## A father's promise

Mark Finley tells a story about a father and son who live in the earthquake-prone country of Armenia. This father took his young son to school one day, and as he left, he promised that he would come back for him when the school day was over. Then a terrible earthquake struck the region. The father ran to the school, hoping his son had survived, but the whole building had collapsed, and his son was buried in the rubble.

However, the father didn't give up. He began tearing away whatever he could of the concrete and twisted iron piled where the school had been. He asked other people to help, and some did for a while, but eventually all of them gave up, doubting they could do enough with their bare hands to save anyone. They told the father he might as well stop digging too, that it was no use, no one could have survived. But he kept right on digging with hands that were bruised and bloodied.

He worked hour after hour without finding anything that suggested any of the children had survived the catastrophe. But still he hoped, so he kept on digging. Then, thirty-six hours after he started digging, he heard the voice he'd been longing to hear. He heard his son say, "Father, I knew you would come! And, Father, there are fourteen other children here too!"

Christ's hands were bruised and bloodied for you and me. He gave up His life for us. He asks that we follow His example of selfless service for others and give God the glory. He asks us to share Jesus and the wonderful Advent message of hope in our work as well as in the rest of our life. He wants us to share with others the truths of eternal value found in God's Word and the Spirit of Prophecy.

God calls us to kneel at the foot of the cross and look to Jesus. He wants us to realize that our weakness becomes strong when we place ourselves in His hands. Paul counseled the Philippians to "let this mind be in you, which was also in Christ Jesus" (Philippians 2:5, KJV). That counsel is meant for us too. As Ellen White put it in *Prophets and Kings*, "Meekness and lowliness are the conditions of success and victory. A crown of glory awaits those who bow at the foot of the cross."[5]

God is calling us to serve Him and others. We're almost home. Jesus is coming soon. We don't have time to waste climbing the earthly pinnacles of success. We need to spend our lives humbly serving for God—giving service that will make a difference. As we lose sight of self and what this world considers success and gain a new vision of Jesus and His care for us, we will find true success.

---

1.   Author unknown.

2.  Cf. White, *The Acts of the Apostles,* 210.
3.  White, *Steps to Christ,* 72.
4.  White, *Steps to Christ,* 70.
5.  Ellen G. White, *Prophets and Kings* (Mountain View, CA: Pacific Press®, 1917), 590.

# CHAPTER 7

# Eliezer, Faithful Servant

One of the landmarks on the campus of the college I attended* is an arch that we students passed under on our way to classes and meals and chapel services. That arch bears the school's motto: "Gateway to Service." In this increasingly secular world, people are tempted to make their decisions based on what the various options they have can do for them, how they can advance their careers or increase their pay or make life easier or bring more pleasure. But my college's motto had it right. As Ellen White put it, "Christ's followers have been redeemed for service. Our Lord teaches that the true object of life is ministry."[1]

World and national events indicate that we're on the verge of a traumatic and climactic time. They tell us that Christ's second advent will happen soon. The universe is watching us. If ever there was a time when people are being called to serve God, it is now!

The apostle Paul told his protégé Titus how we ought to live as Christians. He wrote,

The grace of God that bringeth salvation hath appeared to all men, teaching us that, denying ungodliness and worldly lusts, we should live soberly, righteously, and godly, in this present world; looking for that blessed hope, and the glorious appearing of the

---

* Columbia Union College, which is now named Washington Adventist University.

great God and our Saviour Jesus Christ; who gave himself for us, that he might redeem us from all iniquity, and purify unto himself a peculiar people, zealous of good works.

Our message and mission are clear. God is calling believers to serve by single-mindedly proclaiming Christ, His soon coming, and the three angels' messages. We are not to allow ourselves to be distracted by entertainment, by competitive sports, by wealth, or by the temptation to live an easy lifestyle. This call to give priority to our mission is amplified by the nearness of Christ's coming. The most important way we can serve others is by sharing with them the precious message God has given us.

Selfless service doesn't normally bring people glamour or fame. In fact, it often leads to difficulty and pain. But while those who serve under God's direction may face numerous challenges and problems, they are a great blessing and witness to those whom they serve and to those who witness their faithfulness.

Service to God is so important. A line in a sermon preached by Elder J. R. Spangler, who was then the secretary of the General Conference Ministerial Association, has stuck with me. Elder Spangler said, "Pastors need to be more concerned about their service than their salary." And one of our former General Conference presidents, Elder W. A. Spicer, had the same perspective. He once said, "There are no posts of honor but only of service."

From my childhood on, my father instructed me that it is my wonderful duty to serve God. Of course, God wants us to serve Him because we love Him, not because someone has told us we must. But my father's and mother's concern that I serve God has been a major influence for good in my life. I've found that God will open the way for us to do work for Him if we will step out in faith.

# Five commitments

A life of service is composed of many elements. I believe that to have that kind of life, we must make five specific commitments.

1. *To live a life of Christian service, we must be committed to allowing Christ to be our Master.* That means we must live in obedience to His requirements and commit ourselves to serving Him, recognizing that He is Lord of all and that He has trusted us to be good stewards of the life He has given to us.

2. *To live a life of Christian service, we must be willing to go where God leads us and to trust Him to protect us.* That means we must be willing to ask God every day, "What do You want me to do today?"

3. *To live a life of Christian service, we must be committed to connect with heaven every day.* That means we must have a humble, teachable spirit, and we must commune with God daily through heartfelt prayer and the study of the Bible and the Spirit of Prophecy.

4. *To live a life of Christian service, we must be grateful to God.* That means we must have a deep sense of gratitude to the Omnipotent for His ability and His willingness to care for us, to work in us, and to provide through us the service needed during these last days of earth's history.

5. *To live a life of Christian service, we must be committed to the mission and message of the Advent movement.* That means we must have a deep faith that the Seventh-day Adventist Church has been called to a unique task—that of proclaiming the messages of the three angels of Revelation 14 and of preaching the good news that salvation comes through Christ's righteousness alone.

The Bible contains many stories of people who served God selflessly. One of these stories powerfully and beautifully illustrates these five commitments. It's the touching love story told in Genesis 24.

Usually, when people read this story, they focus on its ending—that romantic moment when Isaac met Rebekah for the first time. However, the main character of the story is a humble man who provided sterling service that God used to accomplish His objectives. This man, Eliezer of Damascus, Abraham's head servant, is the real hero of this story. The lessons of commitment and selfless service this story contains are amazing.

Abraham wanted his son Isaac to marry the right person. After all, the woman he married would become the mother of Israel—and of the promised Messiah. So Abraham's commissioning of Eliezer to find a woman and bring her "home" to marry Isaac laid a heavy burden of responsibility on him. Abraham required Eliezer to swear that he would bring a potential wife for Isaac only from among Abraham's relatives. That Abraham required Eliezer to take this oath emphasizes just how critical the task was. But Abraham also offered Eliezer some assurance. He said that God would send His angel ahead of Eliezer to provide a wife. Then Eliezer walked through the gateway to service, so to speak. He swore that he would do what Abraham asked.

It's obvious that Abraham, the master, trusted Eliezer because Eliezer had proven that he was completely committed to serving Abraham. Similarly, the first of the five commitments God calls us to make is to accept Christ as our Master. God has entrusted a critical mission to us. Are we as committed to serving our divine Master as Eliezer was to serving his human master?

The second commitment God asks us to make is that of trusting God to lead us and to protect us. By this time in his life, Abraham had a strong faith in God's providence, and Eliezer did too. We also see that Abraham had tremendous trust in Eliezer. Can God trust us like that today?

This wonderful story of commitment and service unfolds further. Taking ten camels and many servants, Eliezer headed to the city in Mesopotamia where Abraham's brother, Nahor, lived.

Imagine going to a distant country without having made any prior arrangements and having to find a wife for your boss's son there!

## Eliezer prays

After a difficult and dangerous journey, Eliezer finally arrived at the city. What did he do then? Did he ask people where Nahor lived? Did he try to arrange the outcome of this mission on his own? No, verse 12 tells us he earnestly prayed for God's guidance in choosing a spouse for Isaac.

The third commitment charges us to pray every day. Eliezer relied on his prayer connection with God. "Remembering the words of Abraham, that God would send His angel with him, [Eliezer] prayed earnestly for positive guidance."[2]

Eliezer asked God to guide him to the young woman whom He had in mind for Isaac. He suggested that as the sign that he was talking to the right one, he would ask for a drink, and he prayed that if she was the right one, God would have her offer to draw water for his camels too.

Genesis 24:15 says that before Eliezer finished his prayer, Rebekah came out of the city. When Eliezer saw her, he ran to meet her and asked her for water, and not only did she give him a drink, but she offered to draw water for his camels too.

As we serve the Lord, we're likely we walk into situations that we know little about. Are we as willing to move ahead and to work out the details as we go along as Eliezer was, or do we hesitate, wanting to have everything arranged before we'll get involved? How willing are we to trust God's leading?

Eliezer gave Rebekah expensive gifts to express his appreciation and, in the Eastern tradition, to show his good intentions. Then he asked who she was and whether her family had room to house him and his companions. Since Eliezer had trusted God completely on this special mission and God had responded in kind, Eliezer pushed the questions to the max!

Rebekah answered that she was Bethuel's daughter, Nahor's granddaughter, Abraham's great-niece, Isaac's first cousin once removed.* Imagine how excited Eliezer must have been at God's willingness to reward his faith. God will reward those who serve Him today with incredible miracles too.

---

* Here we have an indication of why Abraham wanted Eliezer to find a wife for Isaac from among Abraham's relatives. Rebekah said her father was Bethuel. The "el" in this name is the Hebrew term for God. Abraham wanted Isaac's wife to be a worshiper of God. He was concerned about her influence on the generations that would follow.

Eliezer was overwhelmed! Verse 26 states that he responded in the only appropriate way—he "worshipped the Lord." The fourth commitment calls us recognize with gratitude God's work in our life. Christ has brought us salvation and new life—why wouldn't we be grateful?

Mystified by the events, Rebekah ran to her home and told her family everything that had happened. Then Laban, her brother, went out to the well and brought Eliezer to the family home. They prepared a meal for him and the men who had come with him, but Eliezer, still committed to fulfilling his mission, refused to eat until he had explained why he was there.

We see here the depth of Eliezer's commitment to carrying out the mission Abraham had given him. That's the fifth commitment—for us, commitment to the mission and message God has given the Seventh-day Adventist Church. By God's grace, let's have an unquestioning faith in the unique mission of our church. God has called us to proclaim the three angels' messages, which point the world to Christ's righteousness and call people to the true worship of God. Let's give our mission the same kind of priority Eliezer gave his.

Rebekah's family was stunned by Eliezer's story and recognized that what had happened was God's doing. Rebekah's father and brother told Eliezer to take her to be Isaac's wife. At this further confirmation of God's leading, Eliezer worshiped Him again. Then he gave more gifts to Rebekah, and gave some to her brother and mother too.

Then, no doubt realizing that they might never see Rebekah again, the family asked Eliezer for ten days with her before he took her away. But Eliezer's mission wouldn't be completed until he delivered Rebekah to Abraham and Isaac, so he was eager to get moving again (see verse 56).

How do we regard the time we spend in serving God? Are we eager to carry out the mission He's given us, or do we linger along the way?

## Rebekah says Yes

Then the family took what must have been an unusual step for those times. They asked Rebekah herself what she wanted to do. Apparently, she had come to believe that Eliezer was on a special mission that God had initiated, so she said she didn't want to delay him. She wanted to leave immediately. "She believed, from what had taken place, that God had selected her to be Isaac's wife, and she said, 'I will go.' "[3]

The family blessed Rebekah, saying she would be the mother of millions, and they helped her pack her things. Then the search party, which was now a bridal party, headed home. And the story ends with that romantic scene of "love at first sight" when Isaac met Rebekah.

Scripture says nothing more about Eliezer. However, I'm sure that throughout the rest of his life, he maintained his faith in the God who had rewarded his dedicated service. No doubt that mission helped establish the children of Israel more firmly as a people and as worshipers of God. And no doubt it helped prepare the way for Christ's fulfillment of His mission—His coming to this earth to live, die, and rise again to live forever, which sealed the promise that through His grace and our acceptance of Him we can have eternal life.

What if Eliezer hadn't been willing to carry out the difficult mission to which both his earthly master and his heavenly Master called him? What if Eliezer hadn't trusted God so implicitly to protect and guide him? But he did. And just as Eliezer took step after step of service because he trusted the Lord completely, so are we to trust God implicitly at every step of our service to Him. We are to rely completely on Him. He won't fail us. Through the Holy Spirit, He will hover over us and guide and protect us. He has His eye on those who walk through the gateway to service. He has promised to be with us to the end of time.

I enjoy walking. One day as I neared my home after having taken an enjoyable walk, I saw a small bird standing on the shoulder of the narrow country road I had been walking on. It was an eastern bluebird—a small bird that is a beautiful blue with an orange chest.

I expected the bird to fly away as I drew near it, but to my surprise, it stood its ground, refusing to move.

Then I saw a bluebird lying on the road, obviously dead. No doubt these two birds had been flying together when a passing car struck and killed the one in the road.

Using the toe of my shoe, I pushed the dead bird off the road so it wouldn't be squashed by the traffic. The live bird kept its place, watching me.

When I got home, I told Nancy what I'd seen. She's a physical therapist, and one of her patients is an expert ornithologist. When Nancy told this man what had happened, he said, "Bluebirds are monogamous. Many times, if one of a pair is injured or killed, its mate will stay with it, not eating or drinking, until it dies too."

Jesus told His disciples, "Are not two sparrows sold for a farthing? and one of them shall not fall on the ground without your Father. . . . Fear ye not therefore, ye are of more value than many sparrows" (Matthew 10:29–31). "If by faith you cast all your care upon Him who marks the falling of a sparrow, you will not trust in vain. If you will rest upon His sure promises and maintain your integrity, angels of God will be round about you."[4]

Just as that little bluebird stood by its mate, God will stand by our side as we serve Him. But unlike that little bird, God will never die. He is the everlasting Creator—He'll never leave us while we're on a mission of service for Him. He'll see us through to the end as He did Eliezer.

We're almost home. God calls us to a life of service, a life dedicated to helping others prepare to go to that home too. We can respond by committing ourselves to serve Him as our Master, to trust in His leading and protection, to connect with heaven every day through prayer and Bible study, to express our gratitude to God, and to fulfill the mission of the Advent movement, carrying the message of Christ and His righteousness and true worship to a world that needs salvation.

1.    Ellen G. White, *Christ's Object Lessons* (Oakland, CA: Pacific Press®, 1900), 326.

2.    White, *Patriarchs and Prophets*, 172.

3.    Ibid., 173.

4.    Ellen G. White, *Testimonies for the Church* (Oakland, CA: Pacific Press®, 1885), 2:72.

# CHAPTER 8

# Bringing Health to the World

E xodus 15:26 is one of the most powerful health-related verses in the Bible. It's a promise that the Lord made to His people Israel while they were on their exodus from Egypt. He said,

> If thou wilt diligently harken to the voice of the LORD thy God, and wilt do that which is right in his sight, and wilt give ear to his commandments, and keep all his statutes, I will put none of these diseases upon thee, which I have brought upon the Egyptians: for I am the LORD that healeth thee.

What a promise! What a blessing! Wouldn't it be wonderful to have that kind of health? Wouldn't your relatives, your neighbors, and your coworkers want to hear how you became so healthy—and perhaps eventually about the God who cares so much about us that He makes promises like this one?

As Seventh-day Adventists, we know how to avoid many of the diseases that inconvenience and even incapacitate people around us. What responsibilities does that lay upon us as individuals? As churches? As a denomination? How are we to help the world?

To get the perspective that the past offers, let's take a brief look at the experience of the Israelites. As we contemplate our role in this world, let's see what we can learn from the story of their journey to the Promised Land.

Chapters 14 and 15 of Exodus record the incredible events surrounding God's deliverance of the Israelites from Pharaoh and the Egyptian army. The people were jubilant. They also knew whom to credit. Exodus 14:31 says, "Israel saw that great work which the Lord did upon the Egyptians: and the people feared the Lord, and believed the Lord, and his servant Moses."

Let's analyze this verse. Israel saw with their own eyes the "great work" that was done for them. They saw that it was the Lord who did this work. The Israelites respected the Lord—in fact, they *believed* Him, which it is absolutely critical for us in God's church today to do also. And the Israelites also believed God's servant Moses. They trusted God's prophet—another important point for us as God's church today.

Two-thirds of Exodus 15 is composed of triumphal songs that Moses and the children of Israel sang to the Lord. One song refers to the power of God's "right hand"—verse 6 trumpeting, "Thy right hand, O LORD, is become glorious in power: thy right hand, O LORD, hath dashed in pieces the enemy."

Interestingly, in discussing the church's mission, Ellen White compared medical missionary work to a hand:

The medical missionary work must be as closely connected with the work of the gospel ministry as the hand and arm are connected with the body. You need the gospel ministry to give prominence and stability to the medical missionary work; and the ministry needs the medical missionary work to demonstrate the practical working of the gospel. The Lord would have His work carried forward symmetrically and harmoniously. His message must be carried to all parts of the world.[1]

## More lessons from the Exodus

Back to Exodus 15. All the Israelites were excited for a few days—until they realized they were facing another big problem: they were in a desert, and the only water they could find was too bitter to swallow.

Verse 24 says that at this point the people murmured against the prophet, asking, "What shall we drink?"

Three days back, all the Israelites were excited about being freed from their slavery in Egypt—until there was no water to quench their thirst. God's incredible power had been at work when He made a path through the Red Sea, and they had believed in God and His prophet and sang about the God who delivered them. But just three days later they'd gone from triumph to despair. You'd think that the miracle of the Red Sea would have been so fresh in their minds that they would have said, "Let's see what God will do." But no, they murmured. They no longer believed in God or in His prophet.

Verse 25 says that then "the Lord shewed [Moses] a tree, which when he had cast into the waters, the waters were made sweet." We're not told what type of tree it was, nor do we know whether it had chemical properties that physically changed the water from bitter to sweet or whether the Lord directly changed the water Himself. Whatever the case, the point for twenty-first-century Seventh-day Adventists is that when we run into problems while carrying out the mission the Lord has assigned us, if we'll cry out to Him, He'll show us a "tree." He'll show us His power.

Sometimes we Seventh-day Adventists seem to parallel those fickle people. Israel had frequent ups and downs—highs of triumph and then lows of complaining. Aren't we tempted to fall into that cycle too?

Exodus 16 chronicles Israel's next failing—their murmuring because of a dwindling food supply. We won't go into that except to note that first they had grumbled about having something to drink and then about having something to eat. Exodus 15:25 says that when they did, "Moses cried to the Lord." That was the right thing for Moses to do, and it's the right thing for us to do today. It's only in God that we have any power.

This point is underscored by the verse I quoted at the beginning of this chapter—Exodus 15:26, which I introduced as one of the most powerful health-related verses in the Bible, a verse that all of us who are interested in healthy lifestyles and health reform and renewal should consider to be our motto. I'll repeat it here:

> If thou wilt diligently harken to the voice of the LORD thy God, and wilt do that which is right in his sight, and wilt give ear to his commandments, and keep all his statues, I will put none of these diseases upon thee, which I have brought upon the Egyptians: for I am the LORD that healeth thee.

The world is at that point right now. Everything around us is falling apart. We face economic upheavals unseen since the Great Depression, political instability everywhere, strange illnesses like H1N1—the swine flu—that create fear, social and moral decay just about direction we turn, and movements aimed at creating a unified religious system that will not allow for religious liberty to worship God on His seventh-day Sabbath. All these problems create despair, and in light of that, people need hope.

God has called this remnant church to proclaim the last warning message to the world. The Holy Spirit will use the church to present God's great plan of salvation to a world in desperate need of hope—hope in every sense of the word; hope for personal peace today, and hope that Christ will come soon.

People also need clear minds, and so do we. We need clear minds as we work at helping society with our unique approach of combining health care with the promotion of a healthy lifestyle. Ellen White has left us some powerful counsel:

> You need clear, energetic minds, in order to appreciate the exalted character of the truth, to value the atonement, and to place the right estimate upon eternal things. If you pursue a wrong course, and indulge in wrong habits of eating, and thereby weaken the intellectual powers, you will not place that high estimate upon salvation and eternal life which will inspire you to conform your life to the life of Christ.[2]

## Looking for guidance

People today are asking what they should eat and what they should drink and how they should live. At this vital time in earth's history, as the world is careening from one crisis to the next, we can step right in and say along with Paul,

> Know ye not that your body is the temple of the Holy Ghost, which is in you, which ye have of God, and ye are not your own? For ye are bought with a price: therefore glorify God in your body, and in your spirit, which are God's (1 Corinthians 6:19, 20). [And] whether therefore ye eat, or drink, or whatsoever ye do, do all to the glory of God (1 Corinthians 10:31).

Couple those verses with the apostle John's desire for his spiritual children: "Beloved, I wish above all things that thou mayest prosper and be in health, even as thy soul prospereth" (3 John 1:2), and you have the prescription for starting a mighty revival and reformation—a movement that will help society in unprecedented ways to find complete health—physical, mental, social, and spiritual. Ellen White advocated such an approach to evangelism. She said, "It is the divine plan that we shall work as the disciples worked. Physical healing is bound up with the gospel commission. In the work of the gospel, teaching and healing are never to be separated."[3]

You and I can proclaim the three angels' messages of Revelation 14:6–12 through the power of the Holy Spirit. This message of the first angel of Revelation 14 says that the God who turned bitter water to sweet and who provided manna to the hungry is telling the world that a part of the "everlasting gospel" is the health message that He has asked Seventh-day Adventists to share with the world. The health message and health work of Seventh-day Adventists are part and parcel of the three angels' messages.

By the power of the Holy Spirit, let's move our witnessing to the next level. Let's cry to the Lord, asking Him to use us in these last days of earth's history. Let's be part of a new revival and reformation that brings a healthy lifestyle through health reform and medical missionary work.

Reflect on Ellen White's counsel:

As we near the close of time we must rise higher and still higher upon the question of health reform and Christian temperance, presenting it in a more positive and decided manner. We must strive continually to educate the people, not only by our words, but by our practice. Precept and practice combined have a telling influence.[4]

So, let's live what we believe. Let's put into practice the diet, exercise, and lifestyle standards based on the Bible and the Spirit of Prophecy. I don't want to step on toes, but in a practical sense that means let's proclaim and live a vegetarian lifestyle. Let's not quibble about whether Seventh-day Adventists or anyone else should drink red wine; alcohol is simply bad for us, and so is caffeine. Let's implement and promote community service for at-risk young people—and on and on. God wants us to share with the world a high standard of healthful, drug-free living. Through the Holy Spirit's power, let's preach it and teach it and live it.

This Seventh-day Adventist movement, with its origins in the disappointment based on a misinterpretation of Daniel 8:14 and then a new understanding of that verse, is now approximately 165 years old. How long must the world wait till the Lord finishes His work for its inhabitants through His people? Is this movement destined to become merely one more of the many religious denominations? The answer is a resounding No!

These efforts may involve the gentle touch of an optometrist; the prayer of a surgeon before an operation; a physical therapist's encouragement; a nurse's tender care; a public health worker's service during a pandemic; a respiratory therapist's easing of a patient's breathing; a health educator's helping a community through practical presentations of our health principles; a pastor's explaining the relationship between physical and spiritual health; a dentist's encouraging words of assurance after a difficult procedure; a literature evangelist's sharing literature on health and spirituality in the homes of the community; a dietician's personal interest in a patient's progress; a cardiologist's taking time out of a busy practice to lecture at a health expo; a psychologist helping a young person turn away from addictions; a person who has been rejuvenated telling a relative about the benefits of the eight natural remedies and living simply; and a church member's giving a loaf of whole-wheat bread to a neighbor or the giving a glass of pure water to a thirsty person. Medical missionary work is meeting people's needs in a practical way that shows them the love of Jesus.

# Medical missionary work

Years ago, Ellen White wrote, "Medical missionary work has been presented as the entering wedge of present truth. It is by this work that hearts are reached, and those once prejudiced are softened and subdued. This is the work that is to be done today."[5] And "medical missionary work is the pioneer work of the gospel. In the ministry of the word and in the medical missionary work the gospel is to be preached and practiced."[6]

Active church members who are health professionals and who reveal Christ in their work can turn local churches into centers of life and health. Making every church a community health center is one of the least expensive and most effective of preventive health-care approaches. It is what God wants us to do to help people make healthy lifestyle modifications.

God wishes to restore the whole person in all the aspects of his or her life—physical, mental, social, and spiritual. As a church, we do work on developing the spiritual dimension of life, but we may have become somewhat hesitant about proclaiming the clear link between biblical truth and our physical well-being. Do we truly believe that God has given exceptional light to Seventh-day Adventists regarding healthy lifestyles and charged this church to use this light to help the world? Ellen White has counseled us that

every minister of the gospel should be prepared to do practical medical missionary work. The medical missionary work is to be as closely united with the gospel ministry as the arm is united to the body. The reluctance shown to promulgations of the principles of health reform is caused by an unwillingness to deny self. In our large cities, the medical missionary work must go hand in hand with the gospel ministry. It will open doors for the entrance of truth.[7]

To open the way for communicating the gospel in the large cities of the world, we need to use medical missionary work. Doing this special work successfully requires balance and wisdom. Again, from the pen of inspiration:

Health reform, wisely treated, will prove an entering wedge where the truth may follow with marked success. But to present health reform unwisely, making that subject the burden of the message, has served to create prejudice with unbelievers and to bar the way to the truth, leaving the impression that we are extremists. Now the Lord would have us wise and understanding as to what is His will. We must not give occasion for us to be regarded extremists.[8]

Why is it that we are to expand the efforts of this powerful blending of the physical and spiritual ministries as the world becomes more chaotic and we approach Christ's soon return? "I wish to tell you that soon there will be no work done in ministerial lines but medical missionary work."[9]

Medical missionary work is the antidote to the New Age movement, to mysticism, and to pagan philosophies that are part of the last-day deceptions of the devil. We are on the field where Christ and Satan are fighting the final battle of the great controversy between good and evil.

# What will you do?

What will you do for medical missionary work? Will you ask the Holy Spirit to bring revival and reformation to you in your life, your job, your home, and your church? Will you allow the Holy Spirit to work through you to initiate revival and reformation? Don't wait for other church members, church employees, and church leaders. God wants you and the world needs you to take the initiative and step forward with God's plan for the last days.

Health professionals can work with pastors to present health lectures for the public sponsored by the local church, and they can participate with pastors in public evangelistic meetings that incorporate health. Pastors and other church leaders can recognize and champion the concept of a blended ministry, working together under the Holy Spirit's guidance to nurture revival and reformation and make every church a community health center.

I believe that God is renewing His clarion call to Seventh-day Adventists and friends of like mind to ignite a new reformation and revival that touches both the physical and spiritual aspects of our nature. We are not only to live up to the rich heritage of the Seventh-day Adventist health ministry, but also to renew our commitment to innovative approaches to health reform, health promotion, primary health care, and medical missionary work, which will be absolutely instrumental in the last proclamation of this Advent movement. As Ellen White tells us, "The world needs today what it needed nineteen hundred years ago—a revelation of Christ. A great work of reform is demanded, and it is only through the grace of Christ that the work of restoration, physical, mental, and spiritual, can be accomplished."[10]

Christ is coming soon. We are called to spiritual revival and reformation. We are called to humble ourselves before God as we take up Christ's message of hope and judgment found in Revelation. We are called to lift high before the entire world the special messages about health reform and lifestyle change that God has entrusted to us. We are called to live up to the highest standards of the health professions of today, thereby pointing people to the Great Physician, who says, "I will put none of these diseases upon thee—for I am the Lord that healeth thee." Ultimately, He promises to bring complete restoration.

We are called to seek revival and reformation so we can do medical missionary work in every practical way, and in the truest sense of the term. We are called to point people to the true Medical Missionary, Jesus

Christ, the Master Physician, the Savior, and our soon-coming King, who says to us, "I am come that they might have life, and that they might have it more abundantly."

What about you? Are you committed to personal and corporate revival, reformation, and renewal? Are you committed to practical medical missionary work—to developing and running health ministries, which would aim at helping people physically, mentally, socially, and spiritually? Are you committed to pointing people to the Master Physician, who can provide abundant and complete life?

1. Ellen G. White, *Ministry to the Cities* (Hagerstown, MD: Review and Herald®, 2012), 132.

2. White, *Testimonies*, 2:66.

3. Ellen G. White, *The Ministry of Healing* (Mountain View, CA: Pacific Press®, 1905), 141.

4. White, *Testimonies*, 6:112.

5. Ellen G. White, letter 110, 1902.

6. White, *The Ministry of Healing*, 144.

7. Ellen G. White, Manuscript 117, 1901.

8. Ellen G. White, *Selected Messages* (Washington, DC: Review and Herald®, 1980), 3:285.

9. Ellen G. White, *Counsels on Health* (Mountain View, CA: Pacific Press®, 1923), 533.

10. White, *The Ministry of Healing*, 143.

# CHAPTER 9

# Mission to the Cities

esus was about to make His triumphal entry into the ancient capital of Israel. He and a crowd of people were outside of the city. As they came to the crest of a hill overlooking the city, Jesus stopped. There was Jerusalem in all its glory, reflecting the light of the descending sun. The pure white marble of the temple walls and the gold-capped pillars created a dazzling sight. Luke 19:41, 42 records how He reacted as He looked down on the city: "Now as He drew near, He saw the city and wept over it, saying, 'If you had known, even you, especially in this your day, the things that make for your peace! But now they are hidden from your eyes.' "

Jesus wept for the city—for the people of the city. He knew that they would reject His mission and call for His crucifixion. But He didn't become angry or resentful. Instead, He wept. He wept for the people of the city. He wept with unutterable sadness because they would ignore His love. He wept for what was to happen to them because they would reject Him as the Messiah and turn from the truth of His Word. How many of us are weeping with Jesus for the cities of this world? How many of us are, like Jesus, looking with unutterable love upon their inhabitants?

If ever there were a time for us to weep with Jesus for the cities of this world, it is now! Down through the ages, most societies were agrarian and rural. Most people lived in the countryside and sought their livelihood in the soil. That has changed. Now, more people live in the cities than in the rural areas of the world. One estimate indicates that by 2050, approximately 70 percent of the world's projected ten billion people will be living in the cities. Are you weeping for the cities yet? What are you willing to do for the salvation of the people of the cities? Concern for their spiritual well-being was heavy on Christ's heart. It should be on ours too.

Matthew 9:35–38 tells of Jesus' ministry for the urban population:

> Jesus went about all the cities and villages, teaching in their synagogues, preaching the gospel of the kingdom, and healing every sickness and every disease among the people. But when He saw the multitudes, He was moved with compassion for them, because they were weary and scattered, like sheep having no shepherd. Then He said to His disciples, "The harvest truly is plentiful, but the laborers are few. Therefore pray the Lord of the harvest to send out laborers into His harvest."

God calls us to go into the cities of the world where the harvest is plentiful but the laborers are few. God is calling us to have compassion on the multitudes—people for whom He wept. People for whom He died and for whom He intercedes today in the Most Holy Place in the heavenly sanctuary. People for whom He will return in the near future. God calls us to preach the messages of the three angels of Revelation 14. He calls us to proclaim His love, His righteousness, and His warning to a dying world, and He calls us to announce His soon coming. Do you care for the people of the great cities? Are you willing to work for their salvation?

God is waiting for us to carry out the unique mission He has given us, that of upholding before the world the spiritual characteristics praised in Revelation 12:17—keeping the commandments of God and having the testimony of Jesus Christ.

For more than a hundred years God has been asking His people to work the cities using the methods He has revealed to us. The writings of the Spirit of Prophecy are replete with instructions about how the work for the cities is to be done. It is to be a sustainable, careful, and comprehensive work—a work that makes use of every aspect of the church's ministry in its approach to reaching the multitudes of the cities. Those who, with humble hearts, follow His will as they do this task will receive His blessing when they've done what they can.

## A needed reinvigoration

To reinvigorate the church's efforts for those who live in the big cities of the world, Ellen White wrote the following:

> There is no change in the messages that God has sent in the past. The work in the cities is the essential work for this time. When the cities are worked as God would have them, the result will be the setting in operation of a mighty movement such as we have not yet witnessed. . . . As a people we are not half awake to a sense of our necessities and to the times in which we live. Wake up the watchmen. Our first work should be to search our hearts and to become reconverted. We have no time to lose upon unimportant issues.[1]

This is God's message to us today. It tells us how we should respond to the calls for revival and reformation. We are to be reconverted. We are to focus on the important issues God wants His remnant church to address. We are to be completely engaged in our mission to tell the world the Good News. We are to surrender ourselves to the Holy Spirit in devotion and humble submission to the will of God so He can prepare us personally and corporately for doing what He has assigned us to do.

Every aspect of our world—the political, economic, social, and physical—is disintegrating. I believe Jesus must come soon. Let's not get caught up in the devil's trap of questioning when it will be. Let's not join those whom Peter had in mind when he wrote,

> Scoffers will come in the last days, walking according to their own lusts and saying, "Where is the promise of His coming? For

since the fathers fell asleep, all things continue as they were from the beginning of creation." . . . Do not forget this one thing, that with the Lord one day is as a thousand years, and a thousand years as one day. The Lord is not slack concerning His promise, as some count slackness, but is longsuffering toward us, not willing that any should perish but that all should come to repentance (2 Peter 3:3–9).

The fact is that Jesus is coming soon! He Himself repeatedly assured the apostle John that He would. (See Revelation 22:7, 12, 20.)

We are living at the end of time. The signs around us are ominous. So, God is calling for us to be revived and reformed through His Spirit, to live in quiet submission to the Word of God and the Spirit of Prophecy, and to pray earnestly and intensely for the outpouring of the Holy Spirit so we can expand our work in the cities. As I noted above, God has promised that when we do this, we will see "a mighty movement such as we have not yet witnessed."

Let us move forward in our work using Christ's method, which, Ellen White indicated, is the only approach that "will give true success in reaching the people."[2] Mrs. White described that method. She said the Savior

1. "*mingled* with men as One
2. who *desired* their good.
3. He *showed* His sympathy for them,
4. *ministered* to their needs,
5. and *won* their confidence.
6. Then He *bade* them, 'Follow Me.' "[3]

Let's follow Jesus' example so we can lead others to Him.

## Till the Lord returns

Revival and reformation are so important that everything we do until the Lord returns is to be laid on the foundation these two experiences comprise. We need the Lord's power, not our own. As Zechariah 4:6 says, " 'Not by might nor by power, but by My Spirit,' says the LORD of hosts." The Holy Spirit's power is vital for direct outreach to the cities—which are the most challenging bastions of the devil's power. Those who have experienced personal and corporate revival and reformation through the power of the Holy Spirit will be drawn into outreach and evangelism.

Recently I read a draft of an article written by someone who was grateful for the call for revival and reformation but wondered about outreach. Revival and reformation have affected everything the Seventh-day Adventist Church is doing, including our focus on evangelism. There should be no doubt that as a product of revival and reformation, we are calling for the greatest evangelistic outreach for the urban and suburban centers of the world ever seen in our day.

Much valiant work has already been done by churches and conferences in efforts to reach the cities in their territories with the three angels' messages, and God has blessed. Seventh-day Adventist Church entities all over the world have given attention to the challenge of the large cities. However, the work in the cities is not easy, and many times we have given uneven, sporadic, and inconsistent attention to the enormous task entrusted to our church to "work the cities as God would have them worked." That is why as we approach the time of Christ's coming, we are to follow God's lead in launching an all-out evangelistic campaign focusing on the large urban and suburban centers of the world and using every type of outreach possible as outlined in the Bible and the Spirit of Prophecy.

God has called us to witness in the cities. The Spirit of Prophecy, God's practical counsel for His remnant people, indicates that under the guidance of the Holy Spirit we're to use a wide variety of outreach activities. These activities will involve the use of centers of influence, local churches, church members, and teams of young people, all of them involved in a variety of outreach initiatives: literature evangelism; small group outreach; medical missionary work; health lectures; door-to-door missionary work; community services and social work that follow Christ's methods; Adventist Community Services and ADRA; integrated media evangelism; counseling centers, reading rooms, and Adventist Book Centers; Bible studies conducted by lay members, young people, and Bible workers; child evangelism; personal evangelism and witnessing; public evangelism; and many more methods yet to be initiated by the Holy Spirit.

We need pastors and lay people working together. As indicated by the Spirit of Prophecy, pastors and health professionals are to blend their ministries in soul winning, as are denominational organizations and the supporting ministries. We need thousands of church members distributing Christian literature such as *The Great Controversy** that will alert millions of people to the times in which we live.

We need everyone dedicated to a comprehensive and sustained evangelistic outreach that will replicate the urban evangelistic work that was done in the city of San Francisco in the latter part of the nineteenth century and the early part of the twentieth century. In the *Review and Herald* of July 5, 1906, Ellen White wrote,

> During the past few years the "beehive" in San Francisco has been indeed a busy one. Many lines of Christian effort have been carried forward by our brethren and sisters there. These included visiting the sick and destitute, finding homes for orphans and work for the unemployed, nursing the sick, and teaching the truth from house to house, distributing literature, and conducting classes on healthful living and the care of the sick. A school for the children has been conducted in the basement of the Laguna Street meetinghouse. For a time a workingmen's home and medical mission was maintained. On Market Street, near the city hall, there were treatment rooms, operated as a branch of the St. Helena Sanitarium. In the same locality was a health-food store. Nearer the center of the city, not far from the Call building,

---

* Ellen White indicated that *The Great Controversy* is the book she most wished circulated.

was conducted a vegetarian cafe, which was open six days in the week and entirely closed on the Sabbath. Along the water front, ship mission work was carried on. At various times our ministers conducted meetings in large halls in the city. Thus the warning message was given by many.

We need strategic planning done under the guidance of the Holy Spirit for evangelizing every city in every country in every division around the world—planning that will produce that "beehive" of activity.

By God's grace, we need to revive what has been called "a culture of involvement." Let's dedicate our lives, energies, talents, resources, and time to finishing God's work so we can go home! Ellen White says she

> was shown God's people waiting for some change to take place,—a compelling power to take hold of them. But they will be disappointed, for they are wrong. They must act; they must take hold of the work themselves, and earnestly cry to God for a true knowledge of the work.[4]

Let's pray for "a true knowledge of the work" and guidance in initiating the greatest approach to reaching the cities of the world with the three angels' messages of Revelation 14.

Our mission to the cities must be based on biblical principles and Spirit of Prophecy counsel. This approach includes the profound and heaven-inspired plan outlined by Ellen White—one that takes an "in-out" approach to the cities. *Within* the cities, we are to have "centers of influence": churches, health clinics and centers, reading rooms, vegetarian restaurants, community centers, and so on. *Outside* the cities, we are to have "outpost centers": training centers for evangelistic workers, lifestyle health centers, and places where urban evangelistic workers can live or visit to be refreshed in a country setting close to God's second book, the book of nature.

Are we willing to take the steps necessary to put into practice God's plans for the urban centers of the world so that a "mighty movement" will result, or will we turn and run like Jonah? Do you sometimes feel like that hesitant prophet who found himself in the belly of a great fish when he rejected God's call to preach in a big city?

# A real story

The book of Jonah tells us a real story about a real man, a real fish, and a real assignment to go to Nineveh and proclaim the downfall of that city. Don't discount this story and others in the Bible as just symbolic or allegorical. The miracle stories of the Bible are true, and they demonstrate God's authority. Believe in the authenticity of God's Holy Word and of the Spirit of Prophecy. God's Word speaks to us in clear language that shows He is in control and that tells us to follow His instructions. Mrs. White counseled,

> Let us give more time to the study of the Bible. We do not understand the word as we should. . . . When we as a people understand what this book means to us, there will be seen among us a great revival.[5]

God's Word is foundational to all that we accept, believe, and stand for as truth. It is essential to revival and reformation.

Unfortunately, Jonah didn't fully accept God's Word because he was afraid to condemn sin in the capital city of an enemy empire. However, he quickly learned to cry to the Lord "out of the belly of Sheol," as recorded in Jonah 2:2, and God heard his voice. God will hear us too when we cry to Him for help with our mission to the Ninevehs of our day. We'll be able to testify as did Jonah: "You have brought up my life from the pit, O Lord, my God. When my soul fainted within me, I remembered the LORD; and my prayer went up to You, into Your holy temple" (verses 6, 7).

Scripture says the Lord heard Jonah's prayer and He "spoke to the fish and it vomited Jonah onto dry land" (verse 10). The Lord then reiterated the mission that He had given Jonah. " 'Arise,' " He said. " 'Go to Nineveh, that great city, and preach to it the message that I tell you.'

So Jonah arose and went to Nineveh, according to the word of the LORD" (Jonah 3:2, 3).

When, like Jonah, we become afraid and feel like running away from our assignment, we need to remember the Lord and plead with Him in prayer to open the way before us. He will point us in the direction of the urban centers of the world as He did Jonah. The results of Jonah's preaching, blessed by the Holy Spirit, were heart-changing and extensive. The city repented.

But the preacher, Jonah, still had not learned the lesson of feeling compassion for the people of the city, and he was embarrassed when that city wasn't destroyed as he had said it would be. Then he even became more upset about the death of a plant than he was at the prospect of the death of all the people who lived in that city. God challenged Jonah, asking him, "Should I not pity Nineveh, that great city, in which are more than one hundred and twenty thousand persons who cannot discern between their right hand and their left?" (Jonah 4:11).

What about us? God asks us what message we will bring to the millions of people who live in the cities of this world. Do we feel pity toward those who face eternal death, or are we more concerned with our comfort and ease?

What the cities need is a portrayal of Jesus Christ—His eternal, saving love and the plan of salvation He has provided so we can have eternal life. They need to see that an all-knowing God the Father, God the Son, and God the Holy Spirit have existed from eternity past and will live throughout all eternity to come. They need to learn about the righteousness Jesus offers us in place of our sinfulness. They need to hear the messages of the three angels of Revelation 14 and to know that Jesus is coming back to earth soon. And they need to be pointed to the true worship of God and the keeping of His commandments, including the precious seventh-day Sabbath of the fourth commandment, which is an eternal sign of loyalty to Him, and a reminder of His creative power, through which He made this earth in six literal days.

People who live in cities need the sacredness and rest the Sabbath provides. Our Advent message will point to our mortality and warn people about mystical beliefs and spiritualism. It will bring new life through an emphasis on health reform. It will share the magnificent sanctuary message that points to the Lamb of Calvary and to the High Priest who is interceding for us now, as the investigative judgment in the Most Holy Place of the heavenly sanctuary prepares the way for the coming of the Lord.

The message we bring will portray the unique calling of the Seventh-day Adventist Church to be God's humble, remnant people who proclaim with love a prophetic warning message as we unselfishly serve others. It will shield us from ecumenism, giving us the power to proclaim the distinctive, historicist prophetic messages of Daniel and Revelation.

The biblical message we carry to the cities will unite us as a worldwide people and keep us from isolating ourselves from society and from each other. Our message to the citizens of the world is that another city is coming—the New Jerusalem, a city of safety, hope, and refuge where God dwells. It's that the answer to all the woes and difficulties of today's earthly cities is the second coming of Jesus Christ!

# God's call today

God is calling us to work the cities without delay. Note the following words of counsel from the Spirit of Prophecy—the great cry for comprehensive urban evangelism and the use of medical missionary work in our approach to the cities:

- It is in the cities of the nations that the gospel worker finds the greatest impenitence and the greatest need. . . . What God's servants do to warn and prepare men for the day of judgment must be done quickly. The conditions that face Christian workers in the great cities constitute a solemn appeal for untiring effort in behalf of the millions living within the shadow of impending doom.[6]
- As a people we need to hasten the work in the cities, which has been hindered for lack of workers and means and a spirit of consecration. At this time, the people of God need . . . to humble their minds, and

to be attentive to the will of the Lord, working with earnest desire to do that which God has shown must be done to warn the cities.[7]

- Again and again I am instructed to present to our churches the work that should be done in our large cities. . . . Often we have been told that our cities are to hear the message, but how slow we are to heed the instruction. I saw One standing on a high platform with arms extended. He turned and pointed in every direction, saying, "A world perishing in ignorance of God's holy law, and Seventh-day Adventists are asleep."[8]

- I appeal to our brethren who have heard the message for many years. It is time to wake up the watchmen. . . . The burden of the needs of our cities has rested so heavily upon me that it has sometimes seemed that I should die. May the Lord give wisdom to our brethren, that they may know how to carry forward the work in harmony with the will of the Lord. . . . The cities must be worked. The millions living in these congested centers are to hear the third angel's message.[9]

- Get the young men and women in the churches to work. Combine medical missionary work with the proclamation of the third angel's message. . . . Send out into the churches workers who will live the principles of health reform.[10]

- During the night of February 27 [1910], a representation was given me in which the unworked cities were presented before me as a living reality, and I was plainly instructed that there should be a decided change from past methods of working. . . . I urged that companies be organized and diligently trained to labor in our important cities. These workers should labor two and two, and from time to time all should meet together to relate their experiences, to pray, and to plan how to reach the people quickly.[11]

- Henceforth medical missionary work is to be carried forward with an earnestness with which it has never yet been carried. This work is the door through which the truth is to find entrance to the large cities.[12]

- How shall we reveal Christ? I know of no better way . . . than to take hold of the medical missionary work in connection with the ministry. . . . The gospel and the medical missionary work are to advance together. The gospel is to be bound up with the principles of true health reform.[13]

- No line is to be drawn between the genuine medical missionary work and the gospel ministry. These two must blend. They are to be joined in an inseparable union, even as the hand is joined to the body.[14]

# Lessons learned in New York City

As we together develop plans for working the cities under the Holy Spirit's leading, we must keep in mind that Ellen White talked about many cities, but there is one in particular with symbolic importance— New York City. It represents the whole world, since so many nationalities and languages are represented there. It is a great center of finance, trade, art, transportation, fashion, advertising, and media. Ellen White said,

Those who bear the burden of the work in Greater New York should have the help of the best workers that can be secured. Here let a center for God's work be made, and let all that is done be a symbol of the work the Lord desires to see done in the world.[15]

Much work has been done in New York, but we have yet to see that city become "a symbol of the work the Lord desires to see done in the world."

Some people love New York, and others hate it. A graffito I saw there captures the challenge of living and working in the large cities of the world. It said, "Concrete jungle: A hard life." There are many good things and many bad things about New York—as there are about any big city. The point is that multitudes of people live there—people who need Jesus and the hope of the Advent message.

God will bless our plans for evangelism in the cities if we allow the Holy Spirit to lead in our making of those plans, and if we follow the counsel found in the Bible and the Spirit of Prophecy. Taking up those plans is a reason for revival and reformation, for intense prayer, for humility before the Lord. Let us never ignore God's pleading with us about the work for the cities.

The interchanges in the early 1900s between Elder A. G. Daniells, the General Conference president, and Ellen White regarding her call for the church to become serious about evangelizing the cities offers us lessons and warnings. According to the biography written by Arthur L. White, Mrs. White continued to feel burdened for the unsaved of New York and the other cities of the world during the last years of her life. She appealed earnestly for unprecedented commitment to evangelizing the cities,[16] and repeatedly sent messages to Elder Daniells, the General Conference president, asking that the church do more for the cities. In response, the General Conference allocated some funds to city evangelism, with New York City particularly in view. However, Elder Daniells complained about the difficulty of getting qualified workers for the cities, and he didn't engage in the work with full focus.

The lack of enthusiasm frustrated Mrs. White. She complained that the leaders weren't caring for the unworked cities as they should, and she said that something had to be done.

So, Elder Daniells laid out some modest plans for doing evangelism in the cities, and then, since he was in California, he went to Ellen White's home to report about the effort for the cities he was making, thinking that Ellen White would appreciate what he was doing. However, according to Arthur White's biography, Mrs. White "refused to see him! The messenger of the Lord refused to see the president of the General Conference!"[17] Instead, she sent word to him that when he was ready to carry out the work that needed to be done, then she would talk with him.

At that, Elder Daniells finally realized that the church's efforts hadn't measured up to what God wanted the church to do in the cities, and he wrote a humble and contrite letter to Mrs. White. Her response indicates that she believed that Daniells and the other leaders of the church still had a ways to go. She declared,

I am charged with a message to you both [Elder Daniells and

Elder W. W. Prescott*] that you need to humble your hearts before God. Neither Elder Prescott nor Elder Daniells is prepared to direct the work of the General Conference, for in some things they have dishonored the Lord God of Israel. High, pure devotion to God is required of men placed in your position. I am to tell you that neither of you is prepared to discern with clear eyesight that which is needed now. . . . The work in the cities has not yet been carried forward as it should be. Had the president of the General Conference been thoroughly aroused, he might have seen the situation. But he has not understood the message that God has given.[18]

The messages from the Lord shook Daniells. The General Conference finally established a special committee of seventeen people to work on plans for the cities. They gave Elder Daniells a year-long sabbatical from his duties as the president of the General Conference so he could provide leadership for the evangelism to be conducted in the cities. He went to New York City and finally fulfilled what God had intended for him to do, helping launch new initiatives in Seventh-day Adventist city evangelism.

May your heart cry out to God as does mine in behalf of the millions of city dwellers in your division, in your union, in your conference, in your mission or field and around the world. Remember that "when the cities are worked as God would have them, the result will be the setting in operation of a mighty movement such as we have not yet witnessed."

I have full confidence that God will fulfill His promise as we humbly submit our plans to Him and follow the instruction He has given in the Bible and the Spirit of Prophecy. Let us plead with the Holy Spirit for the power to accomplish the task entrusted to us.

What a day it will be when Jesus returns and we join with those who have been saved from the large cities and from the rural areas to ascend with the Lord to the homes that will be ours for eternity! Let us dedicate ourselves to fulfilling our role in God's plans to reach the people of the cities.

* Elder W. W. Prescott was the editor of the *Review and Herald* magazine (now the *Adventist Review*) at that time.

1. Ellen G. White, *Medical Ministry: A Treatise on Medical Missionary Work in the Gospel* (Mountain View, CA: Pacific Press®, 1932), 304.

2. White, *The Ministry of Healing*, 143.

3. Ibid., emphasis added.

4. Ellen G. White, *Christian Service* (Washington, DC: Review and Herald®, 1947), 83.

5. Ellen G. White, *Testimonies to Ministers and Gospel Workers* (Mountain View, CA: Pacific Press®, 1944), 113.

6. Ellen G. White, *Evangelism* (Washington, DC: Review and Herald®, 1946), 25.

7. Ibid., 30.

8. Ibid., 32.

9. Ibid., 34, 35.

10. Ellen G. White, *A Call to Medical Evangelism and Health Education* (Nashville: Southern Publishing Association, 1933), 17.

11. Ibid., 13, 14.

12. Ibid., 17.

13. Ibid., 41, 42.

14. Ibid., 44.

15. White, *Evangelism*, 384.

16. See chapter 18, "America's Cities—the Great Unworked Field," in Arthur L. White, *Ellen G. White: The Later Elmshaven Years, 1905–1915* (Hagerstown, MD: Review and Herald®, 1982), 6:219–230.

17. Ibid., 223, emphasis added.

18. Ibid., 225.

# Nuggets From *Evangelism* on Work for the Cities

- Our manner of working must be after God's order. The work that is done for God in our large cities must not be according to man's devising.

- Your work in New York has been started in right lines. You are to make in New York a center for missionary effort, from which work can be carried forward successfully. The Lord desires this center to be a training school for workers, and nothing is to be allowed to interrupt the work.

- We need a sanitarium and a school in the vicinity of New York City, and the longer the delay in the securing of these, the more difficult it will become.

- It would be well to secure a place as a home for our mission workers outside the city.

- To start medical missionary work in New York will be the best thing that you can do.

- In New York there are many who are ripe for the harvest.

- You should feel a decided responsibility for the work of New York City.

- God wants the work to go forward in New York. There ought to be thousands of Sabbathkeepers in that place, and there would be if the work were carried on as it should be.

*These nuggets were gleaned from pages 385–389 of Ellen G. White's book* Evangelism *(Washington, DC: Review and Herald®, 1946).*

# CHAPTER 10

# Remember Your Name!

ames are so important. Scripture reveals that from the time of Creation itself, God has been interested in names. Have you ever noticed that the Bible gives us several instances of God naming what He had just created? For instance, the Bible says that after creating light, "God called the light Day, and the darkness He called Night" (Genesis 1:5), and He did the same with the firmament ("God called the firmament Heaven" [verse 8]) and water and land ("God called the dry land Earth, and the gathering together of the waters He called Seas" [verse 10]). Of course, at the end of Creation week, the Lord blessed and sanctified the seventh day, and He named it *Sabbath*—"rest."

Significantly, when God created Adam, He gave him the job of naming all the other creatures on the earth. (See Genesis 2.) That was a big responsibility! It tells us something about God—that He was willing to trust human beings to carry out His plans.

Sacred history also reveals God's interest in the names of the people whom He called to serve Him. In some instances He specified the names to be given them before they were born, and others He renamed later in their lives. For example,

- Abraham, the father of the faithful, and his wife, Sarah, were Abram and Sarai until God renamed them.
- After Jacob spent a night of physical and spiritual wrestling, the

Lord gave him the name *Israel,* "God contends"—a name clearly associated with God's own name.

- Though Daniel's captors gave him the name *Belteshazzar,* he kept his Hebrew name, *Daniel,* "God is my judge," which was a standing rebuke—and warning—to the heathen rulers of Babylon and Media-Persia.
- And when Saul, the enemy of Christ, was converted on the road to Damascus, he became *Paul,* an emissary for Christ.

Then, of course, there was the naming of John the Baptist.

While the priest Zacharias was burning incense in the temple, an angel appeared before him, frightening him. The angel calmed the poor man, telling him, "Do not be afraid, Zacharias, for your prayer is heard; and your wife Elizabeth will bear you a son" (Luke 1:13).

Then the angel said,

You shall call his name John. And you will have joy and gladness, and many will rejoice at his birth. For he . . . will also go before Him in the spirit and power of Elijah, "to turn the hearts of the fathers to the children," and the disobedient to the wisdom of the just, to make ready a people prepared for the Lord (verses 13–17).

A few verses later, the Bible notes people's amazement when Zacharias and Elizabeth actually did name their little boy *John* despite there being no precedent for that name in their families. (See Luke 1:59–66.)

*John* means "Jehovah is gracious." God chose that special name because of the special work He would entrust to John—that of being the forerunner of Christ. His name was a continual testimony to the indescribable grace of God, which was demonstrated in His giving His one and only Son so we could be saved. What a wonderful God of love!

First John 4:16 declares, "God is love." God's love shapes our lives and our response to His wonderful law. It is the reason we are in this great Advent movement. It motivates us to tell others about Him. God's love for us exceeds anything we can imagine. Scripture says God loves us with an everlasting love (Jeremiah 31:3). *Patriarchs and Prophets*, the first book in the Conflict of the Ages series, begins with the words "God is love," and *The Great Controversy*, the last book in the series, ends in those three words, "God is love."

## Our name and mission

The mission given to Seventh-day Adventists mirrors that of John the Baptist. Like John, we have been called to prepare people for the Lord's coming. We've been given the special work of proclaiming the messages of the three angels of Revelation 14, lifting up Christ and His righteousness and genuine worship of God. We are to tell the world of the great love of God in providing the hope of salvation through Christ's death on the cross and His ministries of intercession and judgment in the heavenly sanctuary. And as Seventh-day Adventists, we have also been commissioned to be reformers who prepare the way of the Lord. As Malachi 4:5 points out, we are to be modern-day Elijahs, bringing reconciliation in families and communities, turning the hearts of the fathers to the children and vice versa.

God calls us to give our lives in Christlike, selfless service to others. We are to follow what Ellen White called "Christ's method," which she described so beautifully: "The Saviour mingled with men as one who desired their good. He showed His sympathy for them, ministered to their needs, and won their confidence. Then He bade them, 'Follow Me.' "[1]

As was true of Christ and His first-century forerunner, our actions will speak louder than our words. The name *Seventh-day Adventist* should call to mind people who improve the physical, social, mental, and spiritual health of their fellow human beings. We want it to make the public think of people who help those in need in practical ways— with food, shelter, and encouragement, and with visitation in homes and schools and prisons and wherever people are in need. Our humble lifestyle and service to others through various acts of kindness speak volumes regarding the love of God.

Like John, we are to exemplify our name by living the upright, simple, godly lives of people who look forward to Christ's return. Through the sanctifying influence of the Holy Spirit, we should be empowered to pursue wholesome and balanced lives characterized by a healthy vegetarian diet that excludes alcohol and other harmful substances like tobacco and caffeine, modest and becoming dress, a strong work ethic, good time management, and a winsome cheerfulness that will draw people to the Lord. We should choose carefully what we watch, read, and listen to, following Paul's counsel to feed our spirits on only those things that are true, noble, just, pure, lovely, of good report, virtuous, and praiseworthy. (See Philippians 4:8.)

We, like John before us, are to be filled with the Holy Spirit as we announce the soon coming of Christ. We must plead with the Lord for the genuine revival and reformation that comes only through the outpouring of the Holy Spirit in latter-rain proportions. I believe that if we humble ourselves before the Lord, we will see the fulfillment of Joel 2:28—God's promise to pour out His Spirit on all flesh. Under the power of His Holy Spirit, we are to be messengers for the Lord, instructing people in the true worship of God and pointing all to Christ and His righteousness, both as recorded in the books of heaven (*justification*) and as demonstrated in the life of His followers here on earth (*sanctification*).

There's power in the name of the Lord!

## Remember your name!

*Remember your name,* Seventh-day Adventist! That name was born of intensive Bible study. As the believers who formed the Seventh-day Adventist Church studied the Bible, prayed earnestly for truth, and followed where the Holy Spirit led, they discovered the biblical teachings that we hold dear. These dedicated pioneers, in simple faith, took the Bible as it read even when that led them away from some of the teachings that were popular in the churches of their day. We must have the same determination to accept only the clear teaching of God's Word. Ellen White notes, "As in earlier ages, the special truths for this time are found, not with the ecclesiastical authorities, but with men and women who are not too learned or too wise to believe the word of God."[2] We call these precious biblical truths Fundamental Beliefs, and they are just that—fundamental! Our name reminds us of them and encourages us to uphold them.

*Remember your name,* Seventh-day Adventist! The "Seventh-day" half of that name reminds us just who it is that we worship. God created this earth in six literal, consecutive, contiguous, twenty-four-hour days and then declared the next day, the seventh day, to be a day of rest. This holy day reminds us that we are a direct creation of God and not some anomalous, accidental product of impersonal evolutionary processes. When we speak our name, we identify ourselves as believers of this truth that Scripture so clearly teaches!

As Seventh-day Adventists living on the very brink of eternity, we are not to minimize our seventh-day distinctiveness. To the contrary, we are to accentuate it, sounding the trumpet of warning with certainty. Note what Ellen White wrote about attempts to de-emphasize our distinctive beliefs:

I was told that men will employ every policy to make less prominent the difference between the faith of Seventh-day Adventists and those who observe the first day of the week. In this controversy the whole world will be engaged, and the time is short. This is no time to haul down our colors.[3]

She continues:

The Lord has permitted the enemy of truth to make a determined effort against the Sabbath of the fourth commandment. He designs by this means to awaken a decided interest in that question which is a test for the last days. This will open the way for the third angel's message to be proclaimed with power.[4]

The third angel of Revelation 14 shows us that the Sabbath is God's special seal or sign and that in the end times it will serve to identify His faithful people. It also tells us that anyone who substitutes any other day in place of the seventh day as the weekly Sabbath will receive the mark of the beast. That's an indication of how important the Sabbath is to God, and thus how important it should be to us. Realizing this, we mustn't align ourselves with any other religious organization or ecumenical body. We should, of course, show ourselves friendly and treat all people with respect, but we are cautioned that

> there is to be no compromise with those who make void the law of God. It is not safe to rely upon them as counselors. Our testimony is not to be less decided now than formerly; our real position is not to be cloaked in order to please the world's great men. They may desire us to unite with them and accept their plans, and may make propositions in regard to our course of action which may give the enemy an advantage over us. "Say ye not, A confederacy, to all them to whom this people shall say, A confederacy" (Isaiah 8:12). While we should not seek for controversy, and should not needlessly offend, we must present the truth clearly and decidedly, and stand firm to what God has taught us in His Word. You are not to look to the world in order to learn what you shall write and publish or what you shall speak.[5]

The Bible tells us that if we believe in the Lord our God, we shall be established, and if we believe His prophets, we shall prosper (see 2 Chronicles 20:20).

*Remember your name,* Seventh-day Adventist! Just as "Seventh-day" reminds us of our origin, "Adventist" tells us where we are going. We are waiting and longing for the return of our Lord Jesus Christ, which will end the suffering that sooner or later in this age we all must endure. Christ's second advent is the "blessed hope" of every genuine Seventh-day Adventist.

In a letter the apostle Paul wrote to the Thessalonian believers, who were new converts to Christianity, he gave more details of this blessed hope. He said,

> The Lord Himself will descend from heaven with a shout, with

the voice of an archangel, and with the trumpet of God. And the dead in Christ will rise first. Then we who are alive and remain shall be caught up together with them in the clouds to meet the Lord in the air. And thus we shall always be with the Lord. Therefore comfort one another with these words (1 Thessalonians 4:16–18).

The promise of Jesus' advent is such an integral part of who we are that it constitutes half our name. So those worshiping in our churches should hear frequent references to our conviction that Jesus is coming soon, that we are almost home! We should be known as people who are expectantly awaiting the return of our Creator and Redeemer. We ought to tell the public that we are awaiting the literal return of the King of kings, who will take us home to heaven.

The powerful name God has given us, *Seventh-day Adventists,* is a three-word sermon of hope. It points to God as the Author and Finisher of our faith. It uplifts Christ in all His beauty and faithfulness. It assures us that the One whom we worship will finally end forever the great controversy that has brought so much suffering to so many people.

*Remember your name,* Seventh-day Adventist! Those who named our church considered many options. And when someone suggested *Seventh-day Adventist,* they believed God said Yes! That He regarded it as the best of the lot. In addressing some people's hesitancy to use our distinctive name, Mrs. White confirmed its origin. She wrote, "We are Seventh-day Adventists. Are we ashamed of our name? We answer, 'No, no! We are not. It is the name the Lord has given us. It points out the truth that is to be the test of the churches.' "[6]

Every time we say our name, we preach a sermon. So, we should avoid abbreviating our name to just Adventist or SDA. Every time we say, "I am a Seventh-day Adventist," we preach a sermon—or perhaps more accurately, several sermons.

So we shouldn't hide our identity when we're naming our churches, institutions, and organizations by inventing some generic, nondistinctive name to use in place of *Seventh-day Adventist.* Instead, we should boldly say who we are, and with that name preach biblical truths to everyone who passes by.

Some years ago I traveled to Venezuela to celebrate the hundredth anniversary of the Seventh-day Adventist Church's expansion into that country, and from there I went to Puerto Rico to attend a session of the union conference. I was hoping to spend the entire flight home catching up on my e-mail, but God had other plans. He sent a family of four down the aisle to seats around me.

The father, who was seated next to me, said that he was an Ismaili Muslim, told a little about this branch of Islam, and went on to introduce me to the humanitarian work of the Aga Khan Foundation, for which he was a volunteer. Then he asked me what I did.

I told this man that I was a pastor in the Seventh-day Adventist Church. I found that he knew little about Christianity and nothing about Seventh-day Adventists, so I used our name as an entry point to tell him about the seventh-day Sabbath and our Savior, Jesus, and His soon coming. The point is that a brief mention of our name opened up a conversation in which I was able to share many of our wonderful beliefs. *Remember your name!*

## A disappointing General Conference session

There were two items on God's agenda for the 1901 General Conference session: reorganization of the church, and the outpouring of the Holy Spirit, which would empower the church, enabling it to finish the mission God had for His people. The leaders of the church did manage to renovate its structure, establishing for the most part the basic structure we have today, with its levels of individual churches, local conferences, and union conferences. It's a good organizational structure, one that promises to continue to serve us well.

But the church didn't accomplish God's second agenda item, the outpouring of the Holy Spirit. Ellen White saw in a vision she had two years later that "the Holy Spirit was not imparted."[7]

Why?

Ellen White gave three reasons: (1) the leaders who had great light didn't walk in that light—some of the personnel of the General Conference and the Review and Herald—one of the church's publishing houses—were slipping into unbelief; (2) the leaders of the church hadn't turned away from their mistakes of the past, giving instead mere lip service to what God wanted; (3) and the leaders had become proud and were nurturing the desire for power. They "did not humble themselves before the Lord as they should have done."[8]

In that vision, Ellen White saw what God had wanted to happen at the 1901 General Conference session. She saw delegates weeping as the Spirit spoke to their hearts. She saw a deep work of repentance taking place—one of the church's leaders rising and confessing all the bitter feelings he had toward other people who were at that session. She saw him go to them one by one asking for forgiveness, and she saw the people he approached ask him for forgiveness too. Then she saw the revival spread to the whole congregation.

"It was a Pentecostal season," she wrote. "God's praises were sung, and far into the night, until nearly morning, the work was carried on."[9] But then she wrote these dreadful lines:

The words were spoken to me: "*This might have been.* All this the Lord was waiting to do for His people. All heaven was waiting to be gracious." I thought of where we might have been had thorough work been done . . . and an agony of disappointment came over me as I realized that what I had witnessed was not a reality.[10]

God still wants to make this outpouring of the Holy Spirit a reality. When will it happen? To some degree, it's up to us. We can't produce revival and reformation on our own—that's the work of the Holy Spirit. But I believe what the Lord told Solomon is His word to us today too: "If my people, which are called by my name, shall humble themselves, and pray, and seek my face, and turn from their wicked ways: then will I hear from heaven, and will forgive their sin, and will heal their land" (2 Chronicles 7:14).

The prophet Hosea invites us:

Come, and let us return to the LORD; for He has torn, but He will heal us; He has stricken, but He will bind us up. After two days He will revive us; on the third day He will raise us up, that we may live in His sight. Let us know, let us pursue the knowledge of the LORD. His going forth is established as the morning; He will come to us like the rain, like the latter and former rain to the earth (Hosea 6:1–3).

In order for us to proclaim the three angels' messages with power so Jesus can come, we need the latter rain of the Holy Spirit. We need the revival and reformation that the Holy Spirit can give us. We need changed lives.

We, who are called by God's name, can humble ourselves, pray, and seek His face. We can lead others to the foot of the cross, and we can implore God to prepare our hearts and send the latter rain of the Holy Spirit.

Will God be able to give the Holy Spirit to us now as He has wanted to since 1901 and even before? We are told, "The descent of the Holy Spirit upon the church is looked forward to as in the future; but it is the privilege of the church to have it now. We must have it, and heaven is waiting to bestow it."[11]

However, this blessing is not unconditional.

- "It is our work, by confession, humiliation, repentance, and earnest prayer to fulfill the conditions upon which God has promised to grant us His blessing."[12]
- "Let the church arise, and repent of her backslidings before God. Let the watchmen awake, and give the trumpet a certain sound."[13]
- "The church must arouse to action. The Spirit of God can never come in until she prepares the way. There should be earnest searching of heart. There should be united, persevering prayer, and through faith a claiming of the promises of God. We have not the first reason for self-congratulations and self-exaltation. . . . We should humble ourselves under the mighty hand of God."[14]

I believe it is high time that we allow this precious name, Seventh-day Adventist, to represent our true identity as God's remnant people. Now is the time for us to be the human voice through whom God calls people out of spiritual Babylon. In a culture steeped in pluralism, relativism, humanism, and hedonism, God has called Seventh-day Adventists to be a countercultural, end-time movement in which every member, in humble, Christlike confidence, is willing to stand for the right though the heavens fall.

Such a mighty movement is possible only through the power of the Holy Spirit. We, as Seventh-day Adventists, must surrender our pride and die to self as we lift up Jesus as the only hope of humankind. Are we ready to plead in prayer for the revival and reformation that only the Holy Spirit can bring about? Are we truly ready to allow God to do what He has longed for decades to do for His remnant people—to pour out the Holy Spirit and finish the work in this generation?

## My appeal

I appeal to readers who are frustrated, discouraged, or distant from the church or the Lord: *Remember your name!*

I appeal to readers who at times have not followed the prompting of the Holy Spirit or God's guidance in the Bible and the Spirit of Prophecy, but have willfully followed their own way or made politically correct decisions instead of standing courageously for what they knew to be right: *Remember your name!*

I appeal to readers who have neglected regular Bible study and prayer and allowed television, popular music, hobbies, the Internet, video games, interschool sports, and any of a myriad of other things—bad or good—to crowd out time for the Lord: *Remember your name!*

I appeal to readers who have forgotten that practical Christian service is the inevitable expression of their relationship with God: *Remember your name!*

I appeal to readers who find themselves drifting far from the theological center of the Word and the fundamental beliefs of the

Seventh-day Adventist Church: *Remember your name!*

I appeal to readers who are living life in the fast lane with little regard for the church: *Remember your name!*

I appeal to readers who have become stale and fossilized in their Christian experience: *Remember your name!*

I appeal to readers who have drifted into independent groups who are critical of the church and who have taken both other people and tithe with them: *Remember your name!*

I appeal to readers who are bitter or angry because some other member offended them or disagreed with them: *Remember your name!*

Joel tells us that the Lord is saying to us,

> "Turn to Me with all your heart,
> With fasting, with weeping, and with mourning."
> So rend your heart, and not your garments;
> Return to the LORD your God. . . .
> Blow the trumpet in Zion,
> Consecrate a fast.
> Call a sacred assembly;
> Gather the people,
> Sanctify the congregation,
> Assemble the elders. . . .
> Let the priests, who minister to the LORD,
> Weep between the porch and the altar;
> Let them say, "Spare Your people, O LORD." . . .
> Be glad then, you children of Zion,
> And rejoice in the Lord your God;
> For He has given you the former rain faithfully,
> And He will cause the rain to come down for you—
> The former rain,
> And the latter rain. . . .
> "I will pour out My Spirit on all flesh;
> Your sons and your daughters shall prophesy,
> Your old men shall dream dreams,

Your young men shall see visions;
And also on My menservants and on My maidservants
I will pour out My Spirit in those days.
And I will show wonders in the heavens and in the earth. . . .
The sun shall be turned into darkness,
And the moon into blood,
Before the coming of the great and awesome day of the LORD. . . .
And . . . whoever calls on the name of the LORD
Shall be saved.
For in Mount Zion and in Jerusalem there shall be deliverance,
As the LORD has said,
Among the remnant whom the LORD calls" (Joel 2:12–32).

We are living in the days described by the prophet Joel—in the time when the Lord wants to pour out the latter rain of the Holy Spirit. We need to plead with the Lord for the revival and reformation that prepares us to receive the latter rain of the Holy Spirit so we can finish God's work through His power.

We are almost home. Remember your name, Seventh-day Adventists!

1. White, *The Ministry of Healing*, 143.
2. White, *Christ's Object Lessons*, 79.
3. White, *Selected Messages*, 2:385.
4. Ibid., 2:370.
5. Ibid., 2:371.
6. Ibid., 2:384.
7. See White, *Testimonies*, 8:104. The entire vision, titled "What Might Have Been," is recounted on pages 104–106.
8. Ibid.
9. Ibid., 105.
10. Ibid., 105, 106, emphasis added.
11. White, *Evangelism*, 701.
12. White, *Selected Messages*, 1:121.
13. Ibid., 1:126.
14. Ibid.

# CHAPTER 11

# A New Reformation

A while ago I went on a tour of Protestant Reformation sites in Europe. What I heard on that tour deepened my impression that God used humble, simple, dedicated people to bring biblical truth back to the attention of the world. He used people who allowed Him to bring about a reformation in their own lives, which they then shared with the world. He used people who were so dedicated that they considered truth more important than their own safety. In order for us and for our church to experience true reformation, we must, like the Reformers, be committed to lifting Christ up and putting self down. We must have the spiritual gift of humility.

Self-centeredness and pride pose some of the greatest challenges we face in our walk with God and in our church life. We fight them all the time. Self-centeredness separates us from God and from each other. It leads us to strive for power, and it derails God's plans for us and for His church. It brings confusion and distortion. It turns us away from God and our heaven-born mission of proclaiming the messages of the three angels of Revelation 14.

Scripture is clear about how God views this subject. The book of Proverbs makes several comments about it. Solomon warned, "Only by pride cometh contention," and "Pride goeth before destruction, an haughty spirit before a fall," and he counseled, "The fear of the LORD is to hate evil: pride and arrogancy, and the evil way" (Proverbs 13:10; 16:18; 8:13, KJV).

It is only through the power of the Holy Spirit that we can be reborn in Christ and have our selfish, self-seeking, proud hearts changed. The Holy Spirit connects us with Christ and heaven, enabling us to have a new life. He deflates our pride and refocuses our lives, lifting up truth and eternal values. Ellen White warned, "To live for self is to perish. Covetousness, the desire of benefit for self's sake, cuts the soul off from life."[1]

To break self's control of our thinking and our living, we must accept the mind of Christ. We must allow Christ to take full control of us and to reform us so that we act and think like Him. Jesus, our Lord, has set the greatest example of this kind of submission and humility. And no one has portrayed Jesus' adoption of these traits better than Paul did in his marvelous account in Philippians 2.

## The humility of Christ

Paul begins by saying, "Let nothing be done through selfish ambition or conceit, but in lowliness of mind let each esteem others better than himself" (verse 3). What a high standard! In fact, it's so high that we wonder how we can reach it. Paul tells us in verse 5: "Let this mind be in you which was in Christ Jesus." We are to allow the Lord to control us so fully that we have His mind—His thoughts and values—rather than our own selfish ambitions.

Verse 6 tells us that Jesus began on a high plane—He is God and equal with the Father. Verse 7 shows the divine Jesus taking three steps down toward us: First, He "made Himself of no reputation." He was God, but He didn't allow His divinity to prevent Him from coming to us. Second, He took "the form of a bondservant." And third, He came "in the likeness of men."

Verse 8 shows Jesus, now "in the likeness of men," taking another three humiliating steps downward so He could save us. First, He "humbled Himself." Second, He "became obedient to the point of death." And third, He died "the death of the cross."

Jesus, the King of the universe, chose to die a humiliating and agonizing death on the cross for you and for me. Often today the cross is portrayed as something somehow spiritual and even beautiful. People memorialize it with artistically beautiful crosses of gold encrusted with jewels. But in reality, the cross was an exceedingly cruel instrument of torture and death—rough and stark and terrible. For those who were crucified, death came slowly and painfully. And the humiliation may have been as hard to bear as the physical torture. The crucified hung naked on their crosses, and those crosses stood little taller than the mocking crowds, so their enemies could spit in their faces. The shame and frustration and anger must have compounded the excruciating physical pain. It was a horrible way to die, one that the Romans reserved for the worst of criminals.

What humility and love our Savior exhibited for us when He voluntarily suffered the punishment that was ours so we could have eternal life! No wonder Paul exclaims,

> Therefore God also has highly exalted Him and given Him the name which is above every name, that at the name of Jesus every knee should bow, of those in heaven, and of those on earth, and of those under the earth, and that every tongue should confess that Jesus Christ is Lord, to the glory of God the Father (verses 9–11).

The contemplation of Christ's willingness to give up self in order to provide us with salvation through the shedding of His blood should humble us—reviving us spiritually and moving us to reform our lives so that we begin to resemble the pattern He set for us.

Jesus is our standard. He submitted Himself to the Father—to whatever the Father would allow to happen to Him—so that we could be saved. How willingly, then, should we humble ourselves and submit ourselves to Him and His will for us! Ellen White counsels, "We must have a greater nearness to God. Much less of self and much more of Jesus Christ and His grace must be brought into our everyday life."[2]

In anticipation of the latter rain promised in Joel 2:23 and exemplified in the outpouring of God's Spirit described for us in Acts 2:17–21, we must be prepared to die to self and to allow Christ's mind to be in us. This is the personal reformation that is needed to allow God's work to progress here and throughout the world. It must start in us. We must reflect Christ in purity of belief and lifestyle. His mind—His thoughts and values and standards— must pervade everything we are and do. We must learn to have unquestioning belief in His Holy Word. We must accept His life as the pattern for our life so that we come to reflect Him more and more.

This is all the more essential because we are standing at a great juncture in life and in earth's history. Jesus is coming soon. The prophecies of Matthew, Daniel, and Revelation are being fulfilled before our very eyes. Signs around us tell us that Jesus will come soon.

## A great Reformer's example

On that tour of the sites connected with the Protestant Reformation, we went to Germany, the homeland of Martin Luther, a man through whom God initiated a great reformation. Luther was a man of humility and conviction; a man who believed that the Bible and the Bible alone is authoritative, and that philosophy and human invention and tradition and fanciful explanations of Scripture are not. He believed the Bible when he read in it that people are saved by grace. He believed in righteousness by faith. He believed in God's personal guidance.

Luther said,

> Whatever I do will be done, not by the prudence of men, but by the counsel of God. If the work be of God, who shall stop it? If it be not, who can forward it? Not my will, nor theirs, nor ours; but Thy will, O holy Father, which art in heaven.[3]

He accepted the fact that when human encouragement failed, he could find peace by resting in faith in almighty God. He knew that human beings aren't the authoritative interpreters of the Bible; the Holy Spirit is.

Luther said,

> We cannot attain to the understanding of Scripture either by study or by the intellect. Your first duty is to begin by prayer. Entreat the Lord to grant you, of His great mercy, the true understanding of His word. There is no other interpreter of the word of God than the Author of this word, as He Himself has said, "They shall be all taught of God." Hope for nothing from your own labors, from your own understanding: trust solely in God, and in the influence of His Spirit. Believe this on the word of a man who has had experience.[4]

This great Reformer, who depended upon biblical truth and not human interpretation, stood for God against the powerful and corrupt church in Wittenberg, Augsburg, and Worms. He knew that the struggle he had begun would last for years. " 'My enemies have been able, by burning my books . . . to injure the cause of truth in the minds of the common people, and destroy their souls; for this reason I consumed their books in return. A serious struggle has just begun.' "[5]

When his life was in great danger, he said,

> The papists do not desire my coming to Worms, but my condemnation and my death. It matters not. Pray not for me, but for the word of God. . . . Christ will give me His Spirit to overcome these ministers of error. I despise them during my life; I shall triumph over them by my death.[6]

However, God protected Luther, giving him the time to translate the Bible into the language of the common people of Germany, which enabled them to read it for themselves—a privilege that soon spread throughout the Western world. And it was there in Worms that Luther made his famous stand, saying that our understanding of God and the way to salvation must be based in the Bible and the Bible alone rather than on tradition and human understanding.

Martin Luther made his case powerfully in German, and then the authorities required him to repeat the defense in Latin, hoping to trip him up. But that demand actually worked to his advantage, because hearing him present his position a second time enabled the princes of Germany and others attending the trial to understand it better.

As the Diet was concluding, the spokesman for the authorities said angrily to Luther, " 'You have not answered the question put to you. . . . You are required to give a clear and precise answer. . . . Will you, or will you not, retract?' "[7]

In response, in a shining moment of history, Luther said,

> Since your most serene majesty and your high mightinesses require from me a clear, simple, and precise answer, I will give you one, and it is this: I cannot submit my faith either to the pope or to the councils, because it is clear as the day that they have frequently erred and contradicted each other. Unless therefore I am convinced by the testimony of Scripture or by the clearest reasoning, unless I am persuaded by means of the passages I have quoted, and unless they thus render my conscience bound by the word of God, I cannot and I will not retract, for it is unsafe for a Christian to speak against his conscience. Here I stand, I can do no other; may God help me. Amen.[8]

As history tells us, Martin Luther and his colleagues went on to provide us with the foundation for our great Protestant heritage, the Bible alone as the source of our faith. This principle directs us to look to God's own interpretation of His Word found in the Word itself rather than to the interpretations devised by mere human beings.

# It's not over yet

Ellen White says,

> The Reformation did not, as many suppose, end with Luther.

It is to be continued to the close of this world's history. Luther had a great work to do in reflecting to others the light which God had permitted to shine upon him; yet he did not receive all the light which was to be given to the world. From that time to this, new light has been continually shining upon the Scriptures, and new truths have been constantly unfolding.[9]

I believe God is calling His remnant church, the Seventh-day Adventist Church, to continue the Reformation—to proclaim the pure truths of the Bible. We are to present the gospel truth of Christ's righteousness and the three angels' messages. Much light has been given to Seventh-day Adventists about the final proclamation of this precious, prophetic Advent message. We are to proclaim the pure, simple truth of Scripture and not human ideas and interpretations of what the Bible says.

I believe this renewed reformation that God is calling for is not one imposed by the church but one imposed by the power of the Holy Spirit. God is calling us back to primitive godliness—back to a pure "Thus saith the Lord." We ought to plead with the Holy Spirit for revival, reformation, and the latter rain of the Spirit. Jesus is coming soon—as He promised three times in Revelation 22. We must be willing to stand for the Lord in these last days of earth's history.

Martin Luther made his loyalty clear. He declared, "Here I stand, I can do no other; may God help me." We must be willing to continue the Reformation and to stand for biblical truth. We must be willing to stand for the message God has called Seventh-day Adventists to proclaim—the three angels' messages. We must be willing to stand with the prophets of the Bible. We must be willing to stand for Christ though the heavens fall. We must be willing to be filled with the power of the Holy Spirit. We must be willing to let self and pride die and to accept God's plan for us.

While Ellen White was in Basel, Switzerland, in 1885, she spoke the words recorded on page 181 of volume 9 of *Testimonies for the Church*. Though originally addressed to ministers, the words, and the challenge, are fitting for all of us to contemplate, as it calls those who hear or read them to stand in simple truth for the Lord. "Will you, my ministering brethren, grasp the rich promises of God?" she said.

> Will you put self out of sight and let Jesus appear? Self must die before God can work through you. . . . Your wills must die; they must become as God's will. He wants to melt you over and to cleanse you from every defilement. There is a great work to be done for you before you can be filled with the power of God. I beseech you to draw nigh to Him, that you may realize His rich blessing.

Are we willing to let God melt us and cleanse us from every distracting question and concern? Are we willing to follow the example of the great Reformer and defender of the Bible, Martin Luther, and to commit ourselves to truth—to say, like him, "Here I stand, I can do no other"?

We must pray earnestly for the wisdom to understand our role in the proclamation of the three angels' messages during these last days of earth's history just before Christ's coming, and we must pray for the power to proclaim this message. We must also pray for humility, and for the outpouring of the Holy Spirit, and that God will use us to continue the Reformation—to point people to Christ, to His righteousness, His truth, and His coming, which will soon take place.

---

1.   White, *Christ's Object Lessons*, 259.
2.   White, *Selected Messages*, 2:376.
3.   White, *The Great Controversy*, 131.
4.   Ibid., 132.
5.   Ibid., 142.
6.   Ibid., 150, 151 .
7.   Ibid., 160.
8.   Ibid.
9.   Ibid., 148, 149.

# CHAPTER 12

# Faith on Fire!

As we see the signs of Christ's coming intensifying every day, the need for unity amongst God's remnant people—in both supporting and denominational ministries—becomes increasingly evident. Now more than ever before we must take seriously the instruction in Hebrews 10:24, 25, that we should "consider one another in order to stir up love and good works, not forsaking the assembling of ourselves together, as is the manner of some, but exhorting one another, and so much the more as you see the Day approaching."

In our walk with Christ, turning—even the slightest bit—from absolute faithfulness to God and His Word can have disastrous consequences. When Eve turned just slightly from God's Word, she left herself open to the serpent's deceptions. When Lot's wife turned her head for just one forbidden glance at her former home, she lost her life. When the hearts of the children of Israel turned away from the Promised Land and back to Egypt, they lost both their homeland and the land of their exile, dying in the desert. All of these people were at one time faithful to God, but they lost sight of Him and relinquished their reliance on His Word, and as a result, the flame of their faith flickered out.

To encourage believers to find a fidelity stronger than that exhibited by these people, the apostle Paul lists in the book of Hebrews examples of genuine faith (see chapter 11), and he gives critical counsel such as that found in Hebrews 6:12: "Do not become sluggish, but imitate those who through faith and patience inherit the promises." That's God's word to us today too. We mustn't become sluggish in the faith either. Instead, through the indwelling power of God, we must live out the exhortation of Jude 3 to "contend earnestly for the faith" so our faith will burn within us!

*We must contend for the faith in the entertainment we choose.* We live in a time of unprecedented technological innovation. We have virtually unlimited access to an entire world of communication and media that, while it holds great potential for evangelism, is often more harmful than beneficial to our Christian life. We must vigilantly guard the gates to the soul. Philippians 4:8—which charges us to dwell only on those things that are true, noble, just, pure, lovely, of good report, and virtuous—is as true today as it was when Paul wrote it. We must let these biblical principles and the counsels of inspiration guide us in the entertainment we choose.

*We must contend for the faith in our personal relationships.* While we should always be pleasant and friendly to everyone, we must be careful about whom we accept as close companions. Such relationships should be built on the solid foundation of a common faith in God and the truths of His Word. After instructing "do not be unequally yoked together with unbelievers," Paul asks these salient rhetorical questions: "What fellowship has righteousness with lawlessness? And what communion has light with darkness?" (2 Corinthians 6:14). We must choose godly associates who will encourage us in our walk with Christ and with God's help break off any relationships that influence us to do things that are displeasing to Him.

*We must contend for the faith in our behavior.* Today in many parts of the world, society encourages behaviors that the Lord abhors. Promiscuity, homosexuality, violence, vulgarity, overindulgence, greed, and pride are all seen as normal, while lifestyles marked by purity and temperance are ridiculed. We mustn't let that influence us. John recorded the encouragement Jesus offers to those who must live a godly life in an evil world:

If the world hates you, you know that it hated Me before it hated you. If you were of the world, the world would love its own. Yet because you are not of the world, but I chose you out of the world, therefore the world hates you (John 15:18, 19).

What a blessing to know that the Lord never asks us to walk a path He has not walked Himself. What encouragement is ours when we read that

we do not have a High Priest who cannot sympathize with our weaknesses, but was in all points tempted as we are, yet without sin. Let us therefore come boldly to the throne of grace, that we may obtain mercy and find grace to help in time of need (Hebrews 4:15, 16).

The same Jesus who has been where we are and has faced what we face has promised to give us the strength we need to walk with Him victoriously.

*We must contend for the faith through our diligence.* The Bible repeatedly reveals that our God is a God of excellence. For His glory, then, as representatives of His who were originally made in His image and who are being restored to that image, we should strive for excellence in all we do. Scripture records that the governors and satraps of Babylon "sought to find some charge against Daniel concerning the kingdom; but they could find no charge or fault, because he was faithful; nor was there any error or fault found in him" (Daniel 6:4). His integrity and diligence witnessed to the glory of God and won the favor of the king. Complacency, apathy, and mediocrity should never be seen in the life of a Christian.

*We must contend for the faith in our pursuit of scientific knowledge.* Recently, many people have become interested in the relationship of science and Scripture. The Lord wants us to consider all aspects of His creation—everything that biology and geology and psychology and sociology can tell us about the world He made and the creatures He placed upon it. However, we must always keep in mind that because

Satan wants to turn human beings away from understanding the will and works of God, Satan conjures a counterfeit for every truth God has established. Through heavenly inspiration, Ellen White made incredibly pertinent comments on the limits of science.

> To many, scientific research has become a curse. God has permitted a flood of light to be poured upon the world in discoveries in science and art; but even the greatest minds, if not guided by the Word of God in their research, become bewildered in their attempts to investigate the relations of science and revelation.
>
> God is the foundation of everything. All true science is in harmony with His works; all true education leads to obedience to His government. Science opens new wonders to our view; she soars high, and explores new depths; but she brings nothing from her research that conflicts with divine revelation.[1]

As those engaged in scientific pursuits explore the wonders of God's creation—either as students, educators, researchers, or practitioners—they should heed these limits.

*We must contend for the faith in our appearance.* Many people—even people trying to follow Jesus' example—go to extremes on this issue. Some conform entirely to the practice of this world, while others appear to carry the matter of distinguishing themselves from the world in appearance as to be purposely unattractive. Christians should stay away from both of these extremes. Note the inspired balance on this issue found in book 3 of *Selected Messages*: "We do not discourage taste and neatness in dress. Correct taste in dress is not to be despised or condemned."[2] On the other hand, however, "self-denial in dress is a part of our Christian duty. To dress plainly, abstaining from display of jewelry and ornaments of every kind, is in keeping with our faith."[3] Using the principles of Scripture, the counsel of the Spirit of Prophecy, and the example of Jesus, we can choose apparel that will present a balanced witness for the Creator God we serve.

*We must contend for the faith in our stewardship.* God has placed many kinds of resources in our hands. We are to manage them wisely to meet our needs but also to support the mission He has given us. So we should

- Be good stewards of the money God has entrusted to us, faithfully returning the Lord's tithe and giving our freewill offerings.
- Be good stewards of our bodies, caring for them by obtaining and using the eight requirements of health: a balanced vegetarian diet, regular exercise, sufficient water, sunlight, abstention from harmful substances (alcohol, tobacco, and illicit drugs), fresh air, adequate rest, and trust in divine power.
- Be good stewards of our time, making sure that we set aside some special time each day for prayer and study of God's Word, and, as the commandment says, keeping the Sabbath day holy.

Regarding that last point, we need to keep in mind that while we have been given "six days to labor and do all your work, the seventh day is the Sabbath of the Lord your God." Too many Seventh-day Adventists remember that the Sabbath exists but forget to keep it holy. The Sabbath is the seal of God's authority, the memorial of His creative and redemptive power, and a weekly opportunity to draw close to Him. We must resist the temptation to use it merely as free time during which we can do whatever we like. We should instead, through God's power, keep the Sabbath holy by preparing for it beforehand, ceasing our normal activities on this sacred day, worshiping the Lord and fellowshiping with believers in church, ministering to the spiritual needs of others, and enjoying God's marvelous handiwork in nature. If, through the mercies of the Lord, we will follow these simple stewardship practices, we will find enough time, enough money, and enough strength not only to meet our daily needs but also to meet the needs of the cause of God.

*We must contend for the faith in our spiritual revivals.* The March 22, 1887, issue of the *Review and Herald* contained an article by Ellen White, titled "The Church's Great Need." In it she stated, "A revival of true godliness among us is the greatest and most urgent of all our needs. To seek this should be our first work."

I praise the Lord that many Seventh-day Adventists are earnestly seeking the Lord's blessing and praying for a genuine revival and reformation in their lives individually and in the church collectively. But we must remain alert because, as we have noted above, the devil has a counterfeit for every biblical truth. We have been cautioned, both in the Bible and in the Spirit of Prophecy, that in these last days, Satan will unleash false revivals in an effort to deceive, if possible, even the elect.

Ellen White wrote pointedly to the very things we now see happening within our ranks. She said,

> We are in continual danger of getting above the simplicity of the gospel. There is an intense desire on the part of many to startle the world with something original, that shall lift the people into a state of spiritual ecstasy, and change the present order of experience. There is certainly great need of a change in the present order of experience; for the sacredness of present truth is not realized as it should be, but the change we need is a change of heart, and can only be obtained by seeking God individually for His blessing, by pleading with Him for His power, by fervently praying that His grace may come upon us, and that our characters may be transformed. This is the change we need today, and for the attainment of this experience we should exercise persevering energy and manifest heartfelt earnestness.[4]

*We must contend for the faith regarding our confidence in the Spirit of Prophecy.* Some Seventh-day Adventists tend to downplay or even dismiss the counsels of the Spirit of Prophecy. We hear some people saying today that while the writings of Ellen White may have some devotional value, we shouldn't let her "limited nineteenth-century perspective" shape our twenty-first-century understanding of Bible truth. But I believe, and the Seventh-day Adventist Church firmly and unashamedly proclaims, that the Spirit of Prophecy is one of God's greatest gifts to His end-time, remnant people. We must trust the Word of the Lord and follow the counsel of His humble messenger, Ellen White, who has consistently pointed us to the Bible as God's authoritative Word. And we mustn't let anyone—pastor, teacher, administrator, local church leader, or anyone else—undermine our confidence in the Spirit of Prophecy.

Paul counseled the Thessalonians, "Do not quench the Spirit. Do not despise prophecies" (1 Thessalonians 5:19, 20). And specifically regarding the end times, Ellen White warned,

> There will be a hatred kindled against the testimonies [the writings of the Spirit of Prophecy] which is satanic. The workings of Satan will be to unsettle the faith of the churches in them, for this reason: Satan cannot have so clear a track to bring in his deceptions and bind up souls in his delusions if the warnings and reproofs and counsels of the Spirit of God are heeded.[5]

In these last days, some among us—perhaps even some whom we have respected as spiritual leaders—may fall away. For the safety of our souls, we must stay faithful. We must not let the subtle doubts nor the open ridicule of friends and family—or anyone else, for that matter—turn us away from the truth God has sent us through His chosen messenger, Ellen G. White.

# Our need, the Holy Spirit

Remaining faithful would be hard enough if all we faced were occasional external temptations. However, we have a sinful nature, and because of it we absolutely cannot obey God's law apart from the power of the Holy Spirit. Human effort can't enable us to attain the level of spiritual vitality to which God is calling us. But the Lord we serve is able! Christ is both the Author and the Finisher of our faith. Therefore, through His strength alone, let us contend for the faith until we all reach what Ephesians 4:13 calls "the measure of the stature of the fullness of Christ."

The Lord loves us so much that He desires to work not only *for* us, but *in* and *through* us as well. His work *for* us credits us with Christ's righteousness. His work *in* us provides us with the spiritual strength we need to remain faithful. And His work *through* us combined with what He does through other faithful believers carries out His mission of bringing salvation to all those who will accept it.

God has established the Seventh-day Adventist Church as His remnant people whom He has commissioned to proclaim the three angels' messages to every nation, tribe, tongue, and people. We cannot reach this daunting goal while making haphazard efforts. Attaining it will require careful planning and the exertions of both full-time church workers and dedicated lay members. Ellen White has told us very clearly, "The work of God in this earth can never be finished until the men and women comprising our church membership rally to the work, and unite their efforts with those of ministers and church officers."[6]

This combination of efforts is not unique to our time. The Bible reveals that God intended both ancient Israel and the early Christian church to work in the same way. Echoing the Lord's instruction in the Old Testament, the apostle Peter declared, "You are a chosen generation, a royal priesthood, a holy nation, His own special people, that you may proclaim the praises of Him who called you out of darkness into His marvelous light" (1 Peter 2:9). Peter wasn't addressing just the leaders of the Christian church of his day. He was speaking to the entire body of Christ—every member, young and old. Every member of the church bears the sacred responsibility to "proclaim the praises of Him who called you out of darkness into His marvelous light."

I, of course, want to be in right standing with Christ when He returns. But my greatest aspiration next to that is to see Him return in my lifetime. And that could happen! All of the Bible's time prophecies have already been fulfilled. We see the global instability foretold by Christ existing now in both the realm of nature and in the political and moral world. What Paul wrote in Romans 13:11 has never been more relevant than it is today—"knowing the time," we can see that "now it is high time to awake out of sleep; for now our salvation is nearer than when we first believed."

Depending on the Holy Spirit's power, we must all work to bridge the gap between our grand ideals and hopes and the practical things that must be done if we are to finish the work in this generation. And the first step in "finishing the work" is to actually go to work. "We should all be workers together with God. No idlers are acknowledged as His servants. The members of the church should individually feel that the life and prosperity of the church are affected by their course of action."[7]

If you want to have your faith set on fire, roll up your sleeves and through the power of the Holy Spirit work for Christ! Breathe life into your local Sabbath School program by showing up on time and being prepared to discuss what you've learned by studying the week's lesson. Go to the weekly prayer meeting to be encouraged as you see your fellow members interceding for others before God's throne of grace. Give the older members of your church a hand when they need it, and meet some of the truly needy in your area by volunteering at your Community Services center. Carry a supply of evangelistic literature with you wherever you go, and give away appropriate pieces to people you meet. Influence your church for good by attending church business meetings and accepting positions of responsibility, no matter how large or small, when the nominating committee calls. For that matter, be willing to serve on the nominating committee itself!

The leadership of the Seventh-day Adventist Church can't fulfill the Lord's call for the church to be His end-time remnant, nor can any single age group or other demographic within the church. You and I as individuals must go to work for Christ. Again, from that wonderful little book *Christian Service*:

> Everywhere there is a tendency to substitute the work of organizations for individual effort. Human wisdom tends to consolidation, to centralization, to the building up of great churches and institutions. Multitudes leave to institutions and organizations the work of benevolence; they excuse themselves from contact with the world, and their hearts grow cold. They become self-absorbed and unimpressible. Love for God and man

dies out of the soul. Christ commits to His followers an individual work,—a work that cannot be done by proxy. Ministry to the sick and the poor, the giving of the gospel to the lost, is not to be left to committees or organized charities. Individual responsibility, individual effort, personal sacrifice, is the requirement of the gospel.[8]

# Our singular goal, to glorify God

In our walk with Christ, we must genuinely focus on the singular goal of glorifying God. We must spend serious time in daily Bible study and prayer, asking the Lord for the promised outpouring of His Holy Spirit. We must humbly ask the Lord for a revival of spiritual fervor and a reformation of anything in our lives that conflicts with the commands of Scripture and the counsels of the Spirit of Prophecy. And beyond personal renewal alone, we must determine to play an active role in the revival and reformation of God's remnant church, committing ourselves to personal effort and involvement that will help our local church family finish the work that God has entrusted to it. We must become an integral part of the outreach of this Advent movement by supporting and nurturing the evangelistic initiatives of our local church and conference that are Bible and Spirit of Prophecy based.

When we each allow the Holy Spirit to change us into the likeness of Jesus, we will automatically begin doing the work that Jesus has commissioned us to do. In this way His character will be seen in what we do, not merely in what we don't do. Mrs. White describes the result of such a revival in *Christ's Object Lessons:*

When the character of Christ shall be perfectly reproduced in His people, then He will come to claim them as His own.

It is the privilege of *every* Christian not only to look for but to hasten the coming of our Lord Jesus Christ. . . . Were all who profess His name *bearing fruit to His glory,* how quickly the whole world would be sown with the seed of the gospel. Quickly the last great harvest would be ripened, and Christ would come to gather the precious grain.[9]

So, we must let the Lord set our faith on fire. We must join the generation that will allow the Holy Spirit to fully develop the character of Jesus within. We must turn our backs on self and lean entirely upon Christ, saying, "Lord, in my hand no price I bring, simply to Thy cross I cling." When we place ourselves completely at the Lord's disposal, He will do wonders *for* us, *in* us, and *through* us.

We are living in the very tips of the toes of the statue that Nebuchadnezzar saw. Right now some of the last events predicted in the book of Revelation are taking place. The latter rain will soon fall to empower God's people. We're almost home!

Are you willing to commit yourself fully to serving Christ and to uplifting His Holy Word and the Spirit of Prophecy? Are you willing to use your talents to carry the message of salvation to the world around you? Is it your desire to have your faith set on fire by the indwelling power of the Holy Spirit, transforming you into Christ's image and making you an ambassador for Christ to a world that is soon to see Him face to face?

---

1.  Ellen G. White, *The Faith I Live By* (Washington, DC: Review and Herald®, 1958), 321.

2.  White, *Selected Messages*, 3:245.

3.  Ibid.

4.  Ellen G. White, *Review and Herald*, March 22, 1892.

5.  White, *Selected Messages*, 1:48.

6.  Ellen G. White, *Gospel Workers* (Washington, DC: Review and Herald®, 1915), 351.

7.  White, *Christian Service*, 10.

8.  Ibid.

9.  White, *Christ's Object Lessons*, 69, emphasis added.

CHAPTER 13

# Go Forward!

Signs of Christ's coming are increasing in number and intensity every day. Events destructive in nature, great confusion in world politics, the pervasive and compromising activities of ecumenism, the dramatic increase and influence of spiritualism, the deterioration of world economies, the disintegration of societal and family values, the disbelief in the absolute authority of God's holy Word and particularly the Ten Commandments, rampant crime and moral decay, wars and rumors of war, and on and on—all point unmistakably to the climax of earth's history and the Lord's return to take us on the final journey home to heaven.

What a tremendous blessing to know that amidst the uncertainty of the world around us, we can rest with absolute confidence in the unchanging Word of God! Throughout the course of human history, God has preserved His holy Word from relentless satanic attacks, preserving an accurate account of our origins, a reliable record of His provision for our salvation, and a glorious glimpse of our soon-coming deliverance.

With the power of His truth, God has carved the Seventh-day Adventist Church out of this chaotic world. We are to be a peculiar people, God's remnant people—people who bring to the world the truths of Christ and His righteousness, the messages of the three angels of Revelation 14, and the good news of Christ's soon coming.

As Bible-believing Christians who live in the last days of earth's history, we are to be what the apostle Peter called "a chosen generation, a royal priesthood, a holy nation, His own special people, that you may proclaim the praises of Him who called you out of darkness into His marvelous light" (1 Peter 2:9). As God's remnant people who are identified in Revelation 12:17 as those "who keep the commandments of God and have the testimony of Jesus Christ," we have a unique message of hope to deliver—a mandate to proclaim to the whole world the grace of God. As Ellen White put it, "Seventh-day Adventists have been chosen by God as a peculiar people, separate from the world. . . . He has made them His representatives and has called them to be ambassadors for Him in the last work of salvation."[1]

# Identifying characteristics

*The Sabbath.* Scripture says God's last-day people will accept and believe all ten of God's commandments, including the fourth commandment, which calls us to remember the Lord's holy Sabbath day. By observing the seventh-day Sabbath, we show our belief that God created the universe in the beginning, and, our observance of that day in the time of the end will distinguish those who have committed themselves to God from those who bear the mark of the beast—the attempt to keep holy a day that God hasn't set apart as holy.

The messages of each of Revelation 14's three angels are related to the Sabbath. The first angel proclaims "the everlasting gospel" (the righteousness of Christ), saying, "Fear God and give glory to Him, for the hour of His judgment has come; and worship Him who made heaven and earth, the sea and springs of water" (Revelation 14:6, 7). God is the Creator, and He is to be worshiped on His Sabbath day as a sign of our loyalty to Him and to His Word and of our recognition of His creative power.

The second angel proclaims, "Babylon is fallen, is fallen . . . because she has made all nations drink of the wine of the wrath of her fornication" (verse 8). She has corrupted God's commandments and instituted a day of worship other than the seventh-day Sabbath, which is the memorial of God's creatorship recognized in Scripture.

The third angel warns that all those who worship the beast and his image and receive his mark on their forehead or on their hand "will be destroyed with fire and brimstone" (see verses 9–12). Scripture indicates that Sunday worship is closely tied to worshiping the beast and his image. God has chosen its biblical counterpart—the keeping of the seventh-day Sabbath—as the ground on which He will test the allegiance of those who claim to worship Him.

*Salvation.* The third angel closes his proclamation by identifying God's people as those "who keep the commandments of God and the faith of Jesus" (verse 12). Genuine children of God rely wholly on Jesus and their relationship with Him for their salvation. They don't obtain salvation through works but through the grace of Christ. That grace is the promise of God's pardon and the provision of His power—justification and sanctification. What Christ does *for* believers (justifying them daily so their standing with God is what it would be if they had never sinned) can't be separated from what He does *in* them (sanctifying them daily as they submit to Him and allow the power of the Holy Spirit to change them so they become more and more like Jesus). This is the "everlasting gospel" of the first angel's message. It is righteousness by faith.

Since we believe God has commissioned us as Seventh-day Adventists to proclaim the messages of the three angels of Revelation 14, we have more reason to proclaim God's grace than does anyone else! The uniquely Adventist great controversy theme is all about God's grace saving sinners and His power transforming them into His sons and daughters—faithful witnesses who proclaim the three angels' messages with Holy Spirit zeal because they have a living connection with Jesus, the Author and Finisher of our faith.

The atoning blood that Jesus shed on the cross and the atoning ministry that He's carrying out right now in the heavenly sanctuary have but one purpose: the salvation of every repentant sinner. Because of Christ's atoning sacrifice and His high-priestly ministry, we can "come boldly to the throne of grace, that we may obtain mercy and find grace to help in time of need" (Hebrews 4:16). It is this marvelous, powerful, redeeming grace that we have been called to proclaim to a sin-sick world.

Furthermore, only a genuine realization of the depths of God's grace can keep us from falling into one or the other of the two opposite extremes: self-indulgence or self-reliance. That marvelous book *Steps to Christ* puts it this way: "We have no ground for self-exaltation. Our only ground of hope is in the righteousness of Christ imputed to us [justification], and in that wrought by His Spirit working in and through us [sanctification]."[2]

*The Spirit of Prophecy.* Revelation 12:17 reveals another great distinguishing mark of God's remnant people: they will "have the testimony of Jesus Christ," which Revelation 19:10 tells us "is the spirit of prophecy." The same Spirit that moved the holy men of old to write the books that make up the Bible has in these last days raised up a messenger for the Lord. He has given us one of the greatest gifts possible in the writings of the Spirit of Prophecy. Through His humble servant Ellen G. White, God has given us inspired insight into Scripture, prophecy, health, education, relationships, mission, families, and much more. The passage of time hasn't outdated the Bible or made it irrelevant, and the same is true of the testimony of God's end-time messenger.

To receive the benefits of this gift, we must read the books the Spirit of Prophecy has inspired, follow the counsels we find there, and share them with others. And there are so many wonderful books to share, including the one Ellen White indicated she most wished us to distribute: *The Great Controversy.*

The Spirit of Prophecy is one of the identifying marks of God's last-day remnant people, and the counsels it contains are just as applicable today as ever before, because they were given to us by Heaven itself. God's faithful remnant must never make of none effect the precious light given in the writings of Ellen G. White.

# Israel out of Egypt

In Old Testament times, God called a particular family and gave them a message and a destiny. He called them to go on a journey of faith and proclaim God's grace to the world. The children of Israel lived in Egypt some four hundred years and eventually were enslaved by the Egyptians. Working through Moses, Aaron, and Miriam, God miraculously freed His people so they could journey to the land He had promised them—so they could begin to carry out the mission He had given them.

When the ten plagues had so devastated Egypt that the Egyptians were willing to let the children of Israel go, they headed south, and Exodus 13:21 says, "The LORD went before them by day in a pillar of cloud to lead the way, and by night in a pillar of fire." What a wonderful God who leads His people day and night!

The Lord led the Israelites down the west side of the Red Sea, next to the Egyptian desert. Exodus 14:2 says God had Moses tell them that they were to camp by the sea—to "camp before Pi Hahiroth, between Migdol and the sea, opposite Baal Zephon."

My father, who spent almost fifteen years in Egypt, studied the description in *Patriarchs and Prophets* of the place where they camped and the geography of the area, and he found a place that he thought fit Ellen White's description. It was a place where the Israelites had the Egyptian desert to the west of them, a mountain in front of them, the Red Sea to the east, and Egypt behind them. Crossing the sea there would have been very difficult. It would certainly have demonstrated that God was more powerful than the Egyptians.

Exodus 14:5, 6 tells us that Pharaoh regretted letting Israel go and pursued them with "six hundred choice chariots and all the chariots of Egypt." And verse 10 says that when the Israelites heard Pharaoh's army coming, they were so distraught that they chided Moses, asking him if it was "because there were no graves in Egypt, [that] you [have] taken us away to die in the wilderness?" (verse 11).

How can people become afraid when it was so obvious that God was leading them? After all, they had that miraculous pillar of cloud by day and pillar of fire at night—why didn't they trust the Power behind that pillar?

Why do we lose our faith at times? How can we see God's guidance and mercy and feel close to Him, and then, when something goes wrong, blame Him? There are lessons here that we need to learn.

Aware of the people's fear, Moses told them to "stand still, and see the salvation of the LORD, which He will accomplish for you today" (verse 13). Often we are tempted to act on our own impulses without allowing the Lord to guide our steps, but He asks us to stick with Him. To reassure the people of Israel, Moses gave the powerful promise that we should all claim as we approach the culmination of the great controversy between Christ and Satan: "The LORD will fight for you, and you shall hold your peace" (verse 14).

The Lord will fight for us. He will open the way. He will provide victory for His church. But we must trust Him. We must humble ourselves before Him. We must obey Him. And we must follow His leading.

Then, through Moses, God gave a command to the children of Israel—the same command He gives His end-time church today. "The LORD said to Moses, . . . 'Tell the children of Israel to *go forward*' " (verse 15, emphasis added).

When God tells us to go forward, we must go forward.

However, the children of Israel couldn't see the big picture. They had forgotten that God was leading them. We must never forget how God has led this Advent movement in the past, or that He will lead it to victory in the future, to the glory of His name and the vindication of His plan of salvation before the whole universe. We are living at the very end of the great controversy. We are almost home, and God is telling us, "Go forward."

But the children of Israel had the desert to their right, the mountain ahead of them, the Red Sea to their left, and the army of Egypt closing in on them from behind, and they felt trapped. They lost sight of the power of God. All they could see were the swords and shields and chariots of the Egyptian army behind them, and the barriers to their escape on all other sides. Where could they go? What could they do?

We face barriers too—both individually and as a church. For some people, it's the mountain of doubt about the Bible on one side, the desert of liberal interpretation on the other, and armies of spiritual confusion pressing them from behind.

But God says they are a holy nation and a peculiar people, and He commands, "Go forward."

Other people are hemmed in by a mountain of financial difficulty on one side, the desert of family and personal conflicts on the other, and the forces of a misguided, sinful society closing in behind them.

To them the Lord says, "You are my chosen people, go forward."

Still others feel trapped by the mountain of miscommunication on one side, the desert of unrest and confusion at home, at work, at church, and in society, and the forces of emotional conflict and mistrust approaching from the rear.

God says, "Go forward regardless of the circumstances."

## To strengthen their trust

Inspiration tells us that

> God in His providence brought the Hebrews into the mountain fastnesses before the sea, that He might manifest His power in their deliverance and signally humble the pride of their oppressors. He might have saved them in any other way, but He chose this method in order to test their faith and strengthen their trust in Him.[3]

At that point God worked one of His mighty miracles. The cloud God was using to lead Israel moved behind them to protect them from the Egyptian army. Then Moses stretched out his hand, and God created the great Red Sea highway. And then, while the cloud restrained the Egyptians, the Israelites stepped forward in faith into the Red Sea.

Can you imagine the excitement of more than a million people walking down into the sea on a dry road? Picture the children laughing as they saw fish swimming as if in an aquarium!

The pen of inspiration points out in powerful language what we can learn from this story:

> The great lesson here taught is for all time. Often the Christian life is beset by dangers, and duty seems hard to perform. The

imagination pictures impending ruin before and bondage or death behind. Yet the voice of God speaks clearly, "Go forward." We should obey this command, even though our eyes cannot penetrate the darkness and we feel the cold waves about our feet. The obstacles that hinder our progress will never disappear before a halting, doubting spirit.[4]

So, we must look to the almighty God, who can take us through anything we face now or will face in the future. We must never lose our trust in Him. We must always obey His command to "go forward." God will make a way through whatever barriers we may face individually and as a corporate people.

God had a plan for Moses and all of Israel. He has a plan for you and for this church too. Never doubt the destiny of this mighty Advent movement. It is in God's hands. And He has given us prophetic instruction that reveals who wins the great controversy—and, of course, it's God!

When the Israelites had reached the other side of the Red Sea, God allowed the Egyptians to pursue them. Exodus 14:23–30 describes what happened then: the chariots lost their wheels, and the mighty Red Sea swallowed up the entire Egyptian army in complete victory. That's a picture of what happens when we "stand still, and see the salvation of the Lord" (verse 13).

Verse 31 tells us that "Israel saw the great work which the Lord had done in Egypt; so the people feared the Lord, and believed the Lord and His servant Moses." And Exodus 15 records the great victory song sung by Moses and the children of Israel. It begins with these words:

"I will sing unto the Lord, for He has triumphed gloriously! The horse and its rider He has thrown into the sea. The Lord is my strength and song, and He has become my salvation; He is my God and I will praise Him; my father's God, and I will exalt Him" (verses 1, 2).

Brothers and sisters of the Advent movement, we are on a

tremendous journey. We must look only to God for our deliverance. The messenger of the Lord declares, "The path where God leads the way may lie through the desert or the sea, but it is a safe path."[5]

Of course, we can rest assured that Satan will challenge whatever direction God tells us to go, tempting us to go another way. Whenever God says, "Go forward," the devil says, "Step back!" So, as we stand on the edge of our eternal home, the same God who commanded the Israelites to go forward into the Promised Land and not backwards into Egypt is today calling us to go forward and not backwards (see Exodus 14:15).

## God's call to us today

God calls us today to *go forward, not backward!* He calls us to stand for truth though the heavens fall. So, we must turn away from fanatical and loose theologies that undermine the pillars of biblical truth with which our church has been built. The biblical beliefs of the historic Seventh-day Adventist Church will not be moved. They will stand secure to the end of time. Remember what the Spirit of Prophecy has told us:

> What influence is it would lead men at this stage of our history to work in an underhand, powerful way to tear down the foundation of our faith—the foundation that was laid at the beginning of our work by prayerful study of the Word and by revelation? . . .
>
> We are God's commandment-keeping people. . . . Every phase of heresy has been brought to bear upon us, to becloud our minds regarding the teaching of the Word—especially concerning the ministration of Christ in the heavenly sanctuary, and the message of Heaven for these last days, as given by the angels of the fourteenth chapter of Revelation. Messages of every order and kind have been urged upon Seventh-day Adventists, to take the place of the truth which, point by point, has been sought out by prayerful study, and testified to by the miracle-working power of the Lord. But the waymarks which have made us what we are, are to be preserved, and they will be preserved, as God has signified

through His Word and the testimony of His Spirit. He calls upon us to hold firmly, with the grip of faith, to the fundamental principles that are based upon unquestionable authority.[6]

*Go forward, not backward!* Let Scripture be its own interpreter. Our church has long held to the historical-biblical or historical-grammatical method of understanding Scripture—allowing it to interpret itself line upon line, precept upon precept. One of the most sinister attacks against the Bible comes from those who believe in the historical-critical method of interpreting it. This approach elevates the authority of people above that of Scripture, saying they are the ones to decide what is truth. Stay away from this approach; it leads people to distrust God and His Word, and it is a deadly enemy of our theology and mission.

Ellen White spoke directly to this issue.

> When men, in their finite judgment, find it necessary to go into an examination of scriptures to define that which is inspired and that which is not, they have stepped before Jesus to show Him a better way than He has led us. . . .
>
> Let not a mind or hand be engaged in criticizing the Bible. . . .
>
> Cling to your Bible, as it reads, and stop your criticisms in regard to its validity, and obey the Word, and not one of you will be lost.[7]

*Go forward, not backward!* Accept the Spirit of Prophecy as one of the greatest gifts given to the Seventh-day Adventist Church—one meant for us today as well as for the past, and one that will be even more important in the future. While we believe the Bible to be the final arbiter of truth, the Spirit of Prophecy provides clear, inspired counsel to help us apply that truth correctly. The Spirit of Prophecy is a heaven-sent guide God has given to instruct us as to how we are to carry out the commission He has given us. It is a reliable expositor of the theology of Scripture. The Spirit of Prophecy is to be read, believed, applied, and promoted. It is not to be used as a club with which to beat people, but it is to be regarded and employed as a marvelous blessing to direct God's church in the last days of this earth's history. Let me repeat a conviction of mine: there is nothing antiquated or archaic about the Spirit of Prophecy; God meant it to help us today and on until Christ returns.

*Go forward, not backward!* God calls us to make our worship Christ centered and Bible based. While it's true that cultures vary throughout the world, the music and other components of our worship mustn't drift into paganism, becoming so focused on emotion and experience that the focus on the Word of God is lost. Our worship, whether simple or complex, must never become a mere performance; it must turn our attention away from self and the human and exalt only Christ. It's impossible to draw a precise line between what is and what is not appropriate, but the Holy Spirit will help us to make wise decisions about the music we use in our worship.

*Go forward, not backward!* God warns us against succumbing to the mistaken practice—gaining support even in the Seventh-day Adventist Church—of accepting worship and evangelistic-outreach methods merely because they are new and trendy. We must vigilantly test all things according to the supreme authority of God's Word and the counsel with which we have been blessed in the writings of Ellen G. White. We're not to reach out to non-Adventist movements or megachurches that promise spiritual success but build on faulty theology. We're to avoid nonbiblical spiritual disciplines and methods of spiritual formation that are rooted in mysticism, such as contemplative prayer, centering prayer, and the "emerging church" movement in which they are promoted. Instead, we should look to humble Seventh-day Adventist pastors, evangelists, biblical scholars, and departmental directors who can provide evangelistic methods and programs that are based on solid biblical principles and the great controversy theme.

*Go forward, not backward!* Stand firm for a literal reading and interpretation of God's Word. We must always humbly recognize that we are finite, fallen creatures observing the works of an infinite, omnipotent God. There are things in both God's great book of nature and in Scripture that we don't fully comprehend. But that which the Lord in

His mercy has given to us in clear language must not be shrouded in skepticism but must be taken as fact simply because God said it. Ellen White wrote,

> We must be careful lest we misinterpret the Scriptures. The plain teachings of the Word of God are not to be so spiritualized that the reality is lost sight of. Do not overstrain the meaning of sentences in the Bible in an effort to bring forth something odd in order to please the fancy. Take the Scriptures as they read.[8]

So, we mustn't misinterpret the first eleven chapters of Genesis or other parts of Scripture as allegorical or symbolic. The Seventh-day Adventist Church both teaches and believes the biblical record that God created the earth in six recent, literal, consecutive, contiguous, twenty-four-hour days. The Seventh-day Adventist Church will never change its stand or belief regarding that foundational doctrine. To misunderstand or to misinterpret that doctrine is to deny God's Word and to deny the very purpose of the Seventh-day Adventist movement as the remnant church of God called to proclaim the three angels' messages with Holy Spirit power. We mustn't drift into atheistic or theistic evolution. And we must continue to support the prophetic understanding that in the very end of time, the distinguishing characteristic of God's people will be their observance of the seventh-day Sabbath. As Seventh-day Adventist church members, let us all hold ourselves accountable to the highest standards of belief based on a literal understanding of Scripture.

Ellen White gave her last sermon to a General Conference session in 1909. When she had finished speaking, she left the platform, but then she turned around, picked up a large Bible, and with trembling hands held it up before the congregation and said, "Brethren and sisters, I commend unto you this book."[9]

We must stand firm on the foundation of Scripture. As God's "people of the Book," let us read the Bible, live the Bible, teach the Bible, and preach the Bible with power from on high.

GO FORWARD!  |  155

# Go forward

Members of God's remnant church, as we come to the end of time, God is telling us, "Go forward!" Go forward in lifting up Christ and His righteousness and proclaiming God's grace. Go forward in presenting the three angels' messages. Go forward in pleading for revival and reformation. Go forward in following the Bible as it reads. Go forward in reading and adhering to the counsel of the Spirit of Prophecy. Go forward in proclaiming to the world the good news of salvation and the imminent second coming of Jesus Christ.

God's grace is leading people all over the world to go forward. We must hold up the banner of public evangelism at all times. The proclamation of God's grace and the three angels' messages is changing people everywhere. The Holy Spirit is working on the hearts of those who hear this wonderful Advent message through our words and evangelistic witness, through our proclamation of God's grace.

We are a beautifully diverse church that is united in Christ and in this God-given, biblical message. We are an international family from every corner of the globe proclaiming God's grace as we go forward united by the Holy Spirit and our foundational biblical beliefs.

What a precious message we have been commissioned to carry to the world!

What a Creator!

What a Redeemer!

What a High Priest!

What an Advocate!

What a Friend!

What a God!

Soon we'll see that small, dark cloud about half the size of a man's hand. It will grow larger and brighter as it draws near the earth. And seated among the billions of angels that will make up that cloud will be the One we've been waiting for—the King of kings and Lord of lords, Jesus Christ, our Redeemer!

We will look up and say, "This is our God; we have waited for Him."

And Christ will look down and say, "Well done, good and faithful servants. Enter into the joy of your Lord." Then we will rise to meet the Lord in the air to go home to be with Him forever—the beautiful end of the Advent journey!

We're almost home. Now isn't the time to give up. It isn't the time to give priority to what this earth has to offer. It's the time for us to seek the Lord and to give ourselves over to serving Him. God will bless us as we do!

---

1.    Ellen G. White, *Testimonies for the Church* (Oakland, CA: Pacific Press®, 1902), 7:138.
2.    White, *Steps to Christ,* 63. For a clear view of righteousness by faith, read the wonderful pages preceding and following this quotation.
3.    White, *Patriarchs and Prophets,* 290; emphasis added.
4.    Ibid.
5.    White, *Patriarchs and Prophets,* 290.
6.    White, *Selected Messages,* 1:207, 208.
7.    Ibid., 1:17, 18.
8.    Ibid., 1:170.
9.    Arthur L. White, *Ellen G. White,* 6:197.